THE MEN OF THE DEEPS
A JOURNEY WITH NORTH AMERICA'S ONLY COAL MINERS CHORUS

JOHN C. O'DONNELL

THE CAPE BRETONIANA RESEARCH SERIES

CAPE BRETON UNIVERSITY PRESS
SYDNEY, NOVA SCOTIA

IN COOPERATION WITH

THE BEATON INSTITUTE, CAPE BRETON UNIVERSITY

Dedicated, in appreciation and with gratitude,

to The Men of the Deeps,

"The sunlit voices

of the men who work deep in the dark."

Copyright © 2016 John C. O'Donnell

All rights reserved. No part of this work may be reproduced or used in any form or by any means, electronic or mechanical, including photocopying, recording or any information storage or retrieval system, without the prior written permission of the publisher. Cape Breton University Press recognizes fair dealing uses under the *Copyright Act* (Canada). Responsibility for the research and permissions obtained for this publication rests with the author.

This book was made possible, in part, through the Robert J. Morgan Grant-in-Aid Program at the Beaton Institute at Cape Breton University. We are pleased to work with the Beaton Institute and other bodies to develop and promote our cultural resources.

Cover design: Cathy MacLean Design, Chéticamp, NS.
Layout: Mike Hunter, West Bay and Sydney, NS.

First printed in Canada.

Library and Archives Canada Cataloguing in Publication

O'Donnell, John C., 1935-, author
The Men of the Deeps : a journey with North America's only coal miners chorus / John C. O'Donnell.
Includes bibliographical references.
Issued in print and electronic formats.
ISBN 978-1-77206-061-4 (paperback).--ISBN 978-1-77206-062-1 (pdf).--ISBN 978-1-77206-063-8 (epub).--ISBN 978-1-77206-064-5 (kindle)
1. Men of the Deeps--History. 2. Choirs (Music)--Nova Scotia--Cape Breton Island--History. I. Title.

ML421.M534O36 2016   782.509716'95   C2016-905079-3
                                            C2016-905080-7

Cape Breton University Press
PO Box 5300
Sydney, Nova Scotia B1P 6L2
Canada

www.cbupress.ca

Sold and distributed by
Nimbus Publishing
3731 MacKintosh St
Halifax, Nova Scotia B3K 5A5
Canada

www.nimbus.ca

Table of Contents

Acknowledgements	IX
Foreword	XI
Prologue	XVII
Chapter 1 – From out of the deeps let a song pierce the sky	1
Chapter 2 – When you come back, we will be old friends	7
Chapter 3 – The authentic voices of Nova Scotia	24
Chapter 4 – They expose their souls	32
Chapter 5 – From the sunken kingdom	44
Chapter 6 – Mining the musical heritage of Nova Scotia	58
Chapter 7 – Tha Faileadh a' Ghuail...	71
Epilogue	81
Appendix	
1 – Meet The Men of the Deeps	84
2 – The Men of the Deeps Membership 1966-2016	93
3 – Major Events, Concerts and Tours	96
4 – Repertoire of The Men of the Deeps	104
5 – The Men of the Deeps Discography	122
Notes	128
Bibliography	139
About the Author	145

"The Cape Breton coal miner has a heartbeat

        it should not be allowed to die."

                Nina Cohen

Acknowledgements

I am indebted to many friends, family and colleagues without whose support and encouragement this extraordinary journey may not have taken the course which brought me to this point. The inspiration to put it all down in writing was spearheaded by a grant from Cape Breton University's Beaton Institute – and that financial incentive might never have happened had it not been for long-time friend and colleague, now deceased, Robert (Bob) Morgan.

Throughout his career Bob was passionately interested in, and a supporter of, anything "Cape Breton." Because of this passion, he was kind enough to leave a legacy to his beloved Beaton Institute. The Robert J. Morgan Grant-in-Aid Program is intended to assist researchers of Cape Breton-related themes to reach a broader audience through publication by CBU Press and by inclusion in a special Beaton Institute publication series known as Cape Bretoniana.

I wish to acknowledge at the outset Cape Breton University, the Beaton Institute and the late Bob Morgan for the support and encouragement they have given me throughout my journey with North America's only coal miners chorus.

My granddaughter, Clara Maltby, was chiefly responsible for helping me to organize and make sense of the reams of notes, letters, news articles and countless memorabilia scattered through my files. Her organizational skills were invaluable at the outset of this project.

And I am indebted to the readers of my rough text as it progressed over the past several months:

Lionel Doucette and Silver Donald Cameron were particularly helpful. Allister and Fiona MacGillivray, Scott Macmillan and Jennifer Brickenden, Gordon Sheriff, Yogi Muise, Jim MacLellan, Bob Roper, Stephen Muise and Jenn Sheppard, and my good friend, Bob Missen, all passed along helpful hints to aid the flow of the text outlining the progression of this fifty-year journey. Fr. Greg MacLeod and Fr. Dan Doucet, two very special Cape Breton friends, provided me with hospitality – most particularly following those weekly Tuesday night summer concerts at the Cape Breton Miners Museum. Their generosity and admiration for The Men of the Deeps deserves very special recognition.

I also wish to recognize Dr. Richard MacKinnon, Professor of Folklore at Cape Breton University and chair of that department, for his generosity in providing the foreword to this publication. Dr. MacKinnon is also founding director of the Centre for Cape Breton Studies at CBU.

Cape Breton University's Beaton Institute is a jewel and a valuable source for researchers of the island's diverse cultural mosaic. Thank goodness for the encouragement and assistance of Catherine Arseneau, director of the Beaton Institute and also archivist, Jane Arnold, along with Mike Hunter and everyone at CBU Press. This project would not have come to fruition without their valuable advice and input.

Throughout my fifty-year association with The Men of the Deeps my family has been a constant support and encouragement. It is well-known that my commitment to the choir involved almost weekly trips between Antigonish and Glace Bay – a round-trip distance of close to 500 kilometers. That kind of intense commitment would not have been possible without the faithful support and encouragement of my wife and children. I am grateful.

J.C.O'D.

A note from the editors

Responsibility for the writing, research and permissions obtained for this publication rests with the author. Effort has been made to properly credit the sources of images. In a book like this, there may be errors or oversights. CBU Press and our authors do recognize our mutual obligation with respect to rights and permissions and apologize for shortcomings.

Here and there, image quality may be lacking, but such is the nature of historical research and personal memoir. Clippings, copies, old photos and less-than-desirable lighting are all factors in collecting; we have done our best to put such images in the best light possible.

All clippings and photos have been provided by the author except where noted.

Foreword

Coal mining has been an essential part of Cape Breton Island's landscape and culture since at least the early 18th century. As with the British Isles and other regions around the world, Cape Breton was heavily influenced by the Industrial Revolution, which began in the 18th century and continued throughout the 19th and early 20th centuries.[1] The first commercial coal mine in North America began production in Cape Breton, at Baie de Mordienne (now Port Morien), around 1720. Known locally as "the French Mine," this primitive drift mine supplied coal by boat to the burgeoning Fortress of Louisbourg further down the Atlantic coast. A bit later, as geographer Stephen Hornsby notes, "between 1786 and 1827, the [British] Colonial Government and local entrepreneurs alternated in operating a small coal mine at Sydney Mines on the north side of Sydney Harbour."[2] Coal mining was in its infancy in the 18th century; the technology was simple and the Sydney mines only employed "about 50 seasonal workers" who produced no more than 13,000 tons of coal per year.[3]

As the 19th century unfolded, mines expanded throughout Nova Scotia as mining methods became more sophisticated and demand for coal to fuel growing industries, including steamships, steadily increased. Increasingly larger workforces also became more organized. As historian Ian McKay has noted, strikes, labour unrest and struggles for better pay and working conditions became common.[4] Class structure was clearly defined in the industrial landscape. Richard Brown, a 19th-century Sydney Mines coal master, lived in an ornate mansion on a hill overlooking the entrance to Sydney Harbour, while miners and families lived in poorly constructed brick-and-wood row housing in close proximity to the mine.[5]

Lowland Scots and English settlers from the coal fields of the British Isles came to develop Cape Breton mines between 1827 and 1857 when a British-based company, the General Mining Association (GMA), held a monopoly on Cape Breton coal. As historian Del Muise notes, "possessing control of all the coal reserves in the province and fairly strong financial backing in England, the company proceeded to revolutionize the industry in Nova Scotia."[6] While coal is found in Cumberland, Pictou and Inverness Counties in Nova Scotia, Cape Breton recorded the largest single area of coal production in the province.[7]

Mines, railways and wharves were built for the new production processes of large-scale, industrial coal mining. Hornsby describes the typical mining town:

> Like those in GMA rows, most houses had a garden where miners kept a pig, some chickens, perhaps a cow, and grew potatoes

and vegetables. The rest of a typical mining village comprised pit buildings, manager's house, company store, school, several churches, and, off company land, bars and independent stores.[8]

Communities, company housing and grid-patterned streets formed around the pitheads and distinctive traditions of work and leisure emerged throughout the island. Indeed, by the early years of the 20th century with the establishment of steel mills to accompany the island's coal mines, Cape Breton became one of the most highly industrialized communities in Canada.

Muise points out that migration to the Cape Breton industrial communities in the late 19th century was epic: "Between 1871 and 1900, the industrial area grew from a population of 12,246 to 33,258 and between 1901 and 1911 to 57,263. Most of the increase was drawn from the neighboring counties on the island."[9] More people were moving to this part of the world to work the mines and to establish communities – company towns, wherein the mining corporations provided housing, power, water and even the stores where miners bought their food and goods. Companies dominated, if not controlled, life in the mining towns.

A variety of ethnic groups can be found in the various Cape Breton Island mining communities. In the early to mid-19th century the General Mining Association (GMA) brought experienced British miners to open the coal seams, but with the expansion of mining, Cape Breton Scots who moved from rural regions soon came to outnumber the early British miners.[10] At the turn of the 20th century, other groups began to arrive searching for employment as the coal mines ramped up production. These included people from places such as Czechoslovakia, Poland, Italy, Belgium, the Ukraine and Lithuania. Others included Caribbean Blacks, Acadian French and Irish settlers. Indeed, after the town was incorporated on August 7, 1913, many of the town's street names in New Waterford were called after the early Irish settlers: Heelan, Duggan, Mahon, Ellsworth and Clogham.[11]

Geographer Hugh Millward points out that

> there have been over 70 mines [in Cape Breton] throughout the years, each with its engine house, workshops, bunkers, loading facilities and waste tips. Most also spawned a rash of miners' housing and since mine employment reached a high of 12,422 by 1915, the company villages developed into some sizeable towns.[12]

Millward traces the stages of development of Cape Breton's coal mines from primitive to more advanced. The earliest stage was the digging of a drift mine or adit (shaft) into coal seams on cliffs; this hand-quarrying of coal from seams exposed in cliffs or eroded banks was the type of mining done throughout the 18th century.

Later came the development of shallow room and pillar mines from "1790 to 1820 on the north side and 1830 to 1865 on the south side, with a typical mine producing 10,000 tons per annum."[13] As the mining moved inland, it was necessary to dig shallow pits for man-access, ventilation and for coal winding to get the coal to the surface. The third stage was more sophisticated, as deeper single-seam coal mines developed. This was brought on by the introduction of large steam engines that allowed for the digging of deeper pits; it also required the development of steam pumps, better ventilation and an extensive outlay of capital. This lasted from approximately 1830 to 1890 at Sydney Mines and 1865-1900 on the south side.[14] The lower seams onshore/single seam offshore stage, lasted from roughly from the turn of the 20th century to 1950. Many of the Cape Breton coal mines already exploited the coal on the land, and at this point began extending the mines as far as possible out under the Atlantic Ocean, furthering the development of submarine mining. The last phase of mining is marked by the development of longwall techniques, lasting until coal mining ended in Cape Breton at the end of the 20th century. Advanced mechanization and sophisticated equipment was the hallmark of this period.

The mining corporations created "company towns" around the mines by trying to control as much as possible of the housing, water, power and food of the communities. Housed in the Beaton Institute, Cape Breton University, for example, are accounts included in what are known as "Waste books," a form of ledger kept by the companies, grocery tabs or chits kept by local businesses. These records provide an indication of the goods and products bought by the average mining family in the run of a year as the company would list all the purchases of a miner and family in this ledger. At the New Waterford Historical Museum, on the site of the old No. 12 mine, you can find the tab of New Waterford resident Mr. Harry Petrie from July 20, 1918, to July 22, 1918. The family's account was with the Dominion Coal Company Limited's Store No. 14; it lists the kind of food his family purchased at the company store. On July 20, for example, the Petries bought onions, raisins, chow, lard, spuds, flour, sugar, butter, tea, beans, steaks, beef and pork along with soap, ribbons and elastic. All of this cost $11.39. Just two days later, on July 22, Mr. Petrie returned to the store for hose, biscuits, more steaks, and baking powder, onions, stew, cod and butter which cost an additional $2.60. These goods indicate that the miner's wife was baking goods for household usage, tea was a common drink, porridge from oats was most likely a common breakfast food and potatoes were a staple for the dinner table. Beef, pork, stew meat, steaks and codfish, it seems, were also commonly consumed food of the time for the mining family.[15]

Company stores were such a hated symbol that a number of the stores were burned to the ground in frustration during a bitter strike in 1925. In New Waterford, for example, a company store was located at the corner of

Plummer Ave. and Heelan Street.[16] A local term was invented for the company stores: the "Pluck Me." According to the Dictionary of Cape Breton English, this is "a disparaging term for the company store where workers purchased on credit."[17] A mother depicted in the film *The Bay Boy* exclaimed, "Yes, that's what they're called, 'Pluck Me.' And for good reason miners get skinned in those places."[18] The Men of the Deeps sing songs about the Pluck Me stores. The chorus of one reads:

> The Pluck Me Store, the Pluck Me Store,
>
> We have to deal at the Pluck Me Store.
>
> And only a little cash is left
>
> When bills are paid at the Pluck me Store[19]

A related term is the "bob-tailed pay sheet," a term that applies to "a miner's payslip with little or no money left after deductions."[20] Floyd Williston describes this term:

> Credit was extended to all coal-company employees. Weekly purchases were deducted from a miner's wages, along with his rent, coal, light, water, medical, church, and blasting-powder charges—all neatly recorded on a "bobtailed sheet." The miners' pay sheets were so dubbed because of the system of cutting off the bottom to show that the employee had no wages coming to him.[21]

Still, Cape Breton coal mining communities bred resilience, overcoming many struggles to survive and thrive. Strong local organizations such as Rotary, Knights of Columbus, Kiwanis, Army and Navy, Daughters of the British Empire, Royal Canadian Legion, Ancient Order of Hibernians, Cercle Evangeline, United Negro Improvement Association, The Italian Hall and others played significant roles in growing the mining communities. Health care and recreational facilities grew as did many churches as the mining towns developed and attained their own identities. Indeed, it is sometimes reported that the concept of the Canadian healthcare system was founded in the "Check Off" system. Individually and collectively, miners paid for access to doctors and community hospitals.[22]

The spirit of the island's people is enacted in what United Nations, Educational, Scientific and Cultural Organization (UNESCO) calls "intangible cultural heritage," particularly in its stories, songs, rituals and commemorations.[23] An annual celebration, Davis Day, for example, is held each June 11 in honour of coal miner Bill Davis, who was killed by company troops in a confrontation in 1925 during a long, bitter strike. Today the commemoration is held each year in the downtown cores of former mining towns; this past year in 2016, the celebration was held in downtown Glace Bay in front of the Old Town Hall (Glace Bay Museum), with representatives in attendance from the United Mine Workers of America, the Davis family, local clergy and elected officials of the Cape Breton Regional Municipality and provincial and federal governments. A non-denominational church service, speeches, food were all part of this celebration; of course, coal mining songs were sung by The Men of the Deeps who have sung at the Davis Day celebrations for the last fifty years, since the founding of the choir.

By continuing to celebrate this community tradition, mining families express their identity and community spirit by highlighting the turbulent past and the difficulties and challenges faced by their forefathers and mothers. There is a phrase that entered oral tradition at the time of that bitter strike of 1925, "stand the gaff." Besco vice-president J. E. McClurg publicly taunted the striking miners in an interview with Andrew Merkel, Canadian Press correspondent of the day saying:

> Poker game, nothing, we hold all the cards. Things are getting better every day they stay out. Let them stay out two months or six months, it matters not, eventually they will have to come to us. They can't stand the gaff.[24]

This was taken as a slur or an insult by miners who set out to prove that they could indeed "stand the gaff" continuing the fight to improve their work and living conditions. The phrase is still heard on picket lines in Cape Breton as a rallying cry that allows striking workers to withstand whatever tactics or pressure an employer may choose to use in a labour dispute. One commentator says "stand the gaff" became a household phrase in Cape Breton "for generations to come, a challenge to the stubborn spirit of our people."[25] Another points out that this "colloquial insult" became "one of the most memorable statements in Cape Breton labour history."[26]

At a time when Cape Breton coal is no longer mined, The Men of the Deeps, through their songs and stories, continue to express the attitudes and feelings of the people who have lived and worked in Cape Breton mining towns. Cape Bretoners are proud of their mining past and the Men of the Deeps keep alive some of the mining traditions that have played significant roles in the development of this island community. This book by Jack O'Donnell celebrates fifty years of The Men of the Deeps and reflects on the many people and places that have shaped this internationally known miners choir, the only one in North America.

Richard MacKinnon 2016

Richard MacKinnon, PhD, is professor of folklore at Cape Breton University where he is also director of the Centre for Cape Breton Studies. He is former Tier I Canada Research Chair in Intangible Culture.

Fig. 1, 2 – Men of the Deeps, at Expo '67, 1967. Photographer unknown. Reference number: 77-1398-1532. Beaton Institute, Cape Breton University.

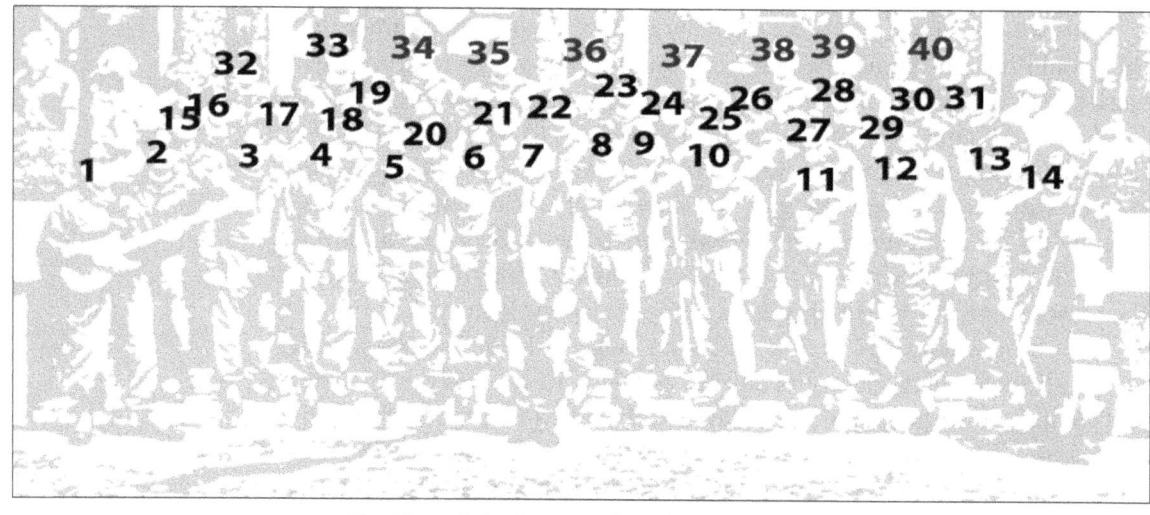

The Men of the Deeps at Expo '67, Montreal

1. Murray Graham
2. Al Provoe
3. Dave Watts
4. Earl Sampson
5. Biff Davis
6. Clark MacKenzie
7. Jack O'Donnell
8. Syd Forgeron
9. Mickey Colson
10. Gerard MacNeil
11. Freeman Jenkins
12. George Merrill
13. Art Martell
14. Gordon LeDrew
15. Bert MacPherson
16. Bob Roper
17. Bill Copland
18. Alec Bezanson
19. Reg Lambert
20. Jimmy P. MacNeil
21. Don Matheson
22. Francis Quan
23. Charlie Sheppard
24. Godfrey Delaney
25. Roy MacLean
26. Francis Delaney
27. John MacLeod
28. Ray Holland
29. Aubrey Martell
30. Gordon Greene
31. Jim MacLellan
32. Francis MacIntosh
33. Ike Lambert
34. Francis MacKenzie
35. Doug Morris
36. Mose Roberts
37. Bob MacLeod
38. Tommy Tighe
39. Myles MacDonald
40. Mike Fleming

Prologue

Whenever The Men of the Deeps choir performs in concert in recent years, it is not unusual for me to take a few moments in the middle of the concert to introduce three of the original members who have been performing with the group for most of the past fifty years. I introduce them as founding members because these three men joined the group in the year of its birth, 1966. In the photo on the page opposite, they are: number 31, Jim MacLellan, number 28, Ray Holland, and number 16, Bob Roper.

I normally introduce Jim MacLellan first, because even though we call him a founding member, his position as Manager of No. 26 Colliery in Glace Bay eventually required that he take a leave of absence from the group for a considerable length of time – from 1972 to 1986. Likewise, with Ray Holland: Because of his commitment to the United Mine Workers of America, District 26 in Cape Breton, Ray also found it necessary to absent himself from the group for much of the period from 1980 to 1994 when he served two separate terms as president of District 26, United Mine Workers of America.

These two gentlemen represent the heart and soul of The Men of the Deeps. Their long-term relationship with the group illustrates a devotion and love of everything that the original organizers of our chorus envisioned when the idea to create a choir composed of genuine working and retired coal miners was conceived. The reality that the occupations of these two men within the mining industry put them at opposite ends of the bargaining table gave further credence to the fact that music and singing are meant to create harmony in the soul. Our audiences love that concept and applaud the notion that a mine manager and a union president can join with the mining industry to create harmony through music.

I usually save the introduction of the third founding member until the audience has absorbed the reality of union and management in harmony.

Bobby Roper has been a singing member (he also plays harmonica) for all of the past fifty years – never having missed a concert season. I suspect there are not too many choirs that can boast that kind of devotion and love for singing. Like all the members in our group, Bobby has seen his share of good and bad times in the mines. In 1952 he was buried in the mine, and following his recovery he returned to work in the same mine in order to get over his fear.[1] It's that kind of commitment to his principles that makes Bobby Roper a very valued member of North America's only coal miners choir.

I was also there in 1966, but I was not the original choir director. That honour lies with a well-known Glace Bay musician of the time, Steve MacGillivray. Steve is now deceased, but his role in the formative days of Cape Breton's Men of the Deeps should not be overlooked and has been well documented in two books by Cape Breton songwriter, author and folk music enthusiast, Allister MacGillivray (no relation to Steve): *Diamonds in the Rough*,[2] published to honour the 25th-anniversary year of The Men of the Deeps in 1991, and *The Men of the Deeps – The Continuing Saga*, published to mark the group's 35th-anniversary year, 2001.[3] Those two publications provide excellent documentation of the first thirty-five year history of The Men of the Deeps.

This 50th-anniversary year publication is not meant to be a history of the chorus. The sequence of chapters does document the chronological history, but my intent as the long-time conductor and musical director of the group is to present my personal reflections on the many interesting and wonderful experiences enjoyed by these worthy ambassadors for Cape Breton and Canada, North America's only coal miners choir, The Men of the Deeps.

Of course, it all began long before I came on the scene. It is to Nina Cohen that full credit should go for the original concept of the Cape Breton Miners' Museum and its offshoot, The Men of the Deeps. Nina, a prominent community leader, activist and philanthropist from Glace Bay conceived the idea in the years leading up to Canada's Centennial Year, 1967. "The Cape Breton coal miner has a heartbeat," she would say, "it should not be allowed to die."

Allister MacGillivray documents Nina Cohen's initial idea that a Miners' Folk Society might be the route to go.[4] Apparently the society boasted of sixty charter members in 1964. I was told of the organiztion when I first met Nina Cohen, but I was never introduced to an active organization known as The Cape Breton Miners' Folk Society.

Inspired by mining culture traditions in Europe, notably Wales, Nina made a wise decision (one of many!) when she asked Myles MacDonald for his advice on bringing to fruition her dream of a miners choir. Mylie, who began his work in the mines of New Waterford at the age of twelve, was a seasoned singer with a network of musical friends in the industrial area of Cape Breton; he seemed the obvious choice to become the first chairman of the Miners' Folk Society. In that capacity, he initiated the process of bringing a group of working and retired miners together to explore the possibility of forming a Cape Breton coal miners choir. The mandate of the society, to promote and encourage the preservation of folk traditions in the mining communities of Cape Breton, would eventually be passed on to the emerging choir.

Initially, Mylie gathered five of his close friends around him and the discussions and planning began. Roy MacLean, George Merrill, Clark MacKenzie, Leslie Lewis, Bob MacLeod and Myles MacDonald would eventually become the nucleus of The Men of the Deeps.[5] Nina's bold ambition was to have a coal miners choir represent Cape Breton at Canada's main centennial celebration, the 1967 World's Fair (Expo '67), in Montreal, and she managed to convince Mylie and many others that this was indeed a possibility. Mylie enlisted the aid of Glace Bay musician, Steve MacGillivray to begin a series of rehearsals, and with the aid of piano accompanist, Gertie

Fig. 3 – Canada's centennial logo.

Fig. 4 – Founding member Bob MacLeod (right) and his brother Alex MacLeod at the Great Wall of China in 1976. Photo courtesy Gordon Sheriff.

Watts, the fledgling choir slowly built up a repertoire of hymns and popular standards. Founding member Bobby Roper remembers singing in the church choir with Mylie, who invited him to join the new forty-member choir.

What made a major impression on me when I accepted Nina Cohen's invitation to "sit in" on a rehearsal of the newly-formed Cape Breton miners chorus in 1966, was the fact that Dr. Helen Creighton was present at that first encounter. I had known of the work of Helen Creighton and was familiar with her early books on folk music in Nova Scotia, but I was still an American citizen in 1966, and having been a permanent resident of Nova Scotia for only four years, I was truly a novice when it came to the broader music scene in Canada. It was Helen's interest in and support of Nina Cohen's dream that really convinced me to accept the challenge presented to me that day. In time, she became a major supporter of my work with The Men of the Deeps and remained an inspiration to me until her death in 1989.

In 1966, Helen had overseen a song-writing contest that had been launched to announce to the world that Cape Breton County's planned centennial project to celebrate Canada's 100th birthday in 1967 would be the building of a permanent Miners' Museum to be located in Glace Bay, and that an offshoot of that project would be the formation of a choir composed of working and retired coal miners. The contest was a huge success and brought in a respectable number of newly composed and (more importantly) newly revised songs that reflected Cape Breton's long association with its coal mining traditions. Song-writing contests were not new to Cape Breton. Radio station CJCB had initiated similar contests at least a decade earlier, and some of the successful songs in those contests, along with songs from The Miners' Folk Society-sponsored contest, eventually found their way into the repertoire of the newly formed choir.

Fig. 5 – Sign announcing proposed construction of the Miners' Museum.

At our first meeting, Helen talked to me about the need to resurrect and bring to life some of the history and traditions of Cape Breton's mining communities. Up to that time, most of her work had taken her to the other end of the province; and what collecting she had done in Cape Breton had focused on the Acadian and Mi'kmaw traditions. She was sure there was a rich song history relating to the mines but to date, it formed only a small part of her collections.

Following our conversation she presented me with a substantial folder containing the results of the contest. Songs like "The Unknown Miner's

Grave," "Kelly's Cove" and "Little Pinkie Engine" which, Helen explained to me, were important references to the past. I was intrigued, and the prospect of bringing a unique male choir to Canada's big celebration in Montreal was an opportunity that I could not pass up.

Those few months leading up to Expo '67 were challenging, but they introduced me to a world that became a major influence on my life. I didn't know it then, but my professional career was destined to follow a radically altered direction.

Fig. 6– Helen Creighten is shown here interviewing Mr. Pierre Chiasson, Grand Etang, 1956. From La Fleur du Rosier, *CBU Press 1986.*

In an effort to upgrade my credentials as a professor of music at St. Francis Xavier University, in 1966 I had applied for and was accepted into a program of graduate studies at the University of London, King's College, in England. And although I was able to be a major part of Nina's dream of bringing the new choir to Expo '67, my early association with The Men of the Deeps was cut short when, in the summer of 1968, I found it necessary to leave the group to take up studies in the United Kingdom. During that period I devoted much of my time to honing my research skills; in particular, my research centred on developments in liturgical music of the 17th and 18th centuries – about as far removed from the area of industrial folk music as one could get! As one recent interviewer put it: "O'Donnell was a trained choral director and pianist who knew more about Gregorian chant than folk music."[6]

I returned to my position at St. Francis Xavier University in the fall of 1970, and for the next two years I was fully immersed in my duties as professor of music. In addition to chairing the department and teaching courses in music theory and the history of music, I regularly performed as pianist with various artists-in-residence. As well, I conducted two choirs at the time: the St. FX University Singers and the St. Ninian's Cathedral choir in Antigonish. And, influenced by the recent directives emanating from the Second Vatican Council to make music and liturgy more accessible to the people, I was also involved in promoting and organizing summer workshops in church music. (For a time, the University even offered a Diploma in Church Music.)

Fig. 7 – Among Helen Creighten's collections of Acadian culture is La Fleur du Rosier, *along with editor Ronald Labelle (CBU Press 1986).*

It was in 1973, with my career focused on my university obligations, that I received a phone call from Ann Terry MacLellan who had recently retired from her successful career as a radio/television personality in Sydney and was now associated with the Cape Breton Development Corporation (DEVCO). In her new capacity as Director of Tourism, she spelled out her

Fig. 8 – And Now the Fields are Green: A Collection of Coal Minings Songs inCanada, *by John C. O'Donnell (CBU Press 1992).*

vision to make The Men of the Deeps choir an arm of DEVCO's plan for tourism on the island. In order to do this, she explained, the crown corporation was interested in having the choir return to its original mandate of promoting and preserving the folk traditions of Cape Breton's coal mining communities. Recalling my original enthusiasm for the subject, she wondered if I might be interested in returning to the group as conductor and musical director.[7]

Reflecting on my earlier discussions with Dr. Helen Creighton, I accepted Terry's invitation to return as musical director and conductor of The Men of the Deeps, and thus began a fascinating journey that brought me into the world of industrial folk traditions from Cape Breton and around the globe.

Throughout the remainder of my career at St. FX, I was able to publish my findings on Cape Breton's industrial folk music traditions in a number of national and international journals. And in 1992, with the assistance of Cape Breton University Press, I completed a major publication on coal mining songs in Canada, *And Now the Fields are Green.*[8] The collection earned endorsements from some of North America's most prestigious scholars in industrial folk music, and it pleased me when folk music icon, Peggy Seeger, in reviewing the collection for the English Folk Music Journal, wrote "I learned so much.... Had I not, as a reviewer, received the book gratis, I would have bought it."[9]

Chapter 1

"From out of the deeps let a song pierce the sky."[1]

The Men of the Deeps choir was introduced to the public on three consecutive nights in 1966: at the Savoy Theatre in Glace Bay on November 1, at Sydney's Vogue Theatre on November 2 and at the Paramount Theatre in New Waterford on November 3. Because its repertoire was comprised of only a few songs at that time, the choir needed an opening act.

At those debut concerts, the choir was partnered with the singing priest, Father Columba McManus. Father McManus was a member of the Servite Friars in Montreal, and his singing career had caught the eye of Nina Cohen as she carefully crafted the birth of Cape Breton's coal miners choir. His contribution to those debut concerts was praised as "most moving" and "very memorable" in an early review which appeared in *The Cape Breton Post*. His "youth, attractive personality and agreeably haunting baritone voice" proved to be a winning combination that complemented the voices of the newly formed coal miners choir. Father McManus's later duties as a member of a religious order were those of a teacher, a retreat master and a counsellor; he was fortunate in his early years as a priest to have the approval of his order to pursue his short career as a singing priest. Father McManus passed away in 2010 at the age of seventy-five.

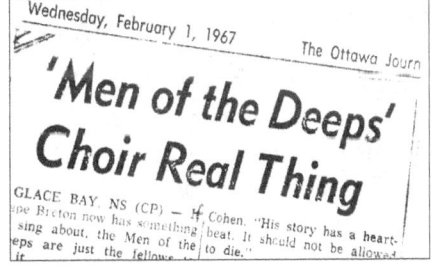

Fig. 1.1 – The Ottawa Journal, *Feb. 1, 1967.*

Fig. 1.2 –
Terry MacLellan
(Ann Terry), ca. 1970.
Photographer unknown.
Reference number:
77-1415-1549. Beaton
Institute, Cape Breton
University.

Fig. 1.3 – Program from the official opening of the Miners' Museum.

Fig. 1.4 – Cape Breton Miners' Museum, Glace Bay, NS.

The November performance at Sydney's Vogue Theatre resembled a Hollywood red carpet event, with Ann Terry MacLellan of CJCB Radio doing interviews with dignitaries as they arrived. Terry, as she was known to her close friends, brought much dignity to the evening. She eventually became a close friend and supporter of The Men of the Deeps,[2] and in a few years' time she would be responsible for bringing the choir under the financial wing of the Cape Breton Development Corporation (DEVCO).

That *Cape Breton Post* review was titled "An Impressive Debut"[3]; it was kind to the choir's performance: "The Men of the Deeps have yet to arrive, but happily they are on their way...."

More insightful (and perhaps even contentious) was an editorial which appeared in *The Cape Breton Post* on November 4, 1966 – the day following the three opening concerts. The editorial was titled "The very audacity of it." Far from being critical, however, the editorial writer marvelled at the audacity it took to present the miners chorus to the Cape Breton public after only two months of training. "...it takes the boldest sort of venture to make The Men of the Deeps ready for performance at Expo '67 next August. The very audacity of it makes it worthy of respect." The editorial concludes by predicting that "This will be Cape Breton's adventure.... It should inspire us all to stand up and sing! From out of the deeps let a song pierce the sky."[4]

The opening of the Glace Bay Miners' Museum took place on July 31, 1967. It was another gala event which lasted the entire day during which many church and government dignitaries, along with representative leaders from the mining industry paid their respects and lauded result. The morning ceremony even included a "flypast" featuring aircraft from a variety of maritime squadrons.

W. A. (Tony) Boyle, President of the United Mine Workers of America, travelled to Glace Bay from Washington, DC, to bring greetings at the morning ceremony; he also played an important role in the dedication of the Miners' Museum at the luncheon ceremony and the unveiling of the Miners' Memorial Plaque at the evening ceremony. The Canadian government was represented by Hon. Allan J. MacEachen, at that time Minister of Health and Welfare; the new museum was officially opened by the Hon. H. P. MacKeen, Lieutenant Governor of Nova Scotia, and was described as "an historic event" by the *Cape Breton Post*.

Musically, The Men of the Deeps were a small part of the ceremonies with a brief performance at the museum site at the afternoon ceremony during which Nina Cohen unveiled the cornerstone.

The day concluded with a tour of the newly constructed museum, including a visit to the Ocean Deeps Colliery – a mine replica over which the museum was built. Located underground beneath the museum, it illustrates for visiting tourists various types of coal mining and mining techniques. The Ocean Deeps Colliery has served as a location for at least two television productions featuring The Men of the Deeps.

Fig. 1.5 (Above left) – Group photo of the choir in a museum exhibit.

Fig. 1.6 (Above) – Nina Cohen unveils the corner stone of the Miners' Museum.

Fig. 1.7 (Left) – The choir rehearses in the original museum theatre space.

—

The Men of the Deeps had spent the months following the November (1966) debut concerts getting to know themselves and their new director, learning new repertoire and rehearsing for the upcoming big event scheduled to take place on a purpose-built island in the St. Lawrence River at Monteal, the site of Expo '67.

The group prepared a relatively short concert which included some of the prize-winning songs from the 1966 song-writing contest[5] along with some popular male choral arrangements of familiar hymns and show tunes. Ray Holland wrote a song to introduce the group; "The Cape Breton Coal Miners" was set to a familiar American folk tune, "Sweet Betsy from Pike" (better known to the rest of the music world as "Villikens and His Dinah"). Leon Dubinsky, a friend of Nina Cohen and a talented musician and composer well-known in industrial Cape Breton, also offered to put melodies to some of the contest entries. (His version of Helen C. MacDonald's "The Man with a Torch in His Cap" is still in the active repertoire of The Men of the Deeps, fifty years on.)

Among the first "imported" songs relating to the mining industry to find a place in the repertoire of The Men of the Deeps were Merle Travis's haunting "Dark as a Dungeon," and his very popular tune (made famous

LET A SONG PIERCE THE SKY

by Tennessee Ernie Ford), "Sixteen Tons." The two Travis songs, along with "We're All Jolly Wee Miner Men," a catchy little tune that American folklorist George Korson had collected from Bob Stewart (a Glace Bay miner who had been attending a UMWA convention in Washington, DC). Korson published the song in his *Coal Dust On The Fiddle* collection.[6] Later, in the 1980s, Helen Creighton collected another version of the song, "The Jolly Miner." That version also became part of the choir's permanent repertoire. Those two songs, along with another variant, "She Loves Her Miner Lad,"[7] share the distinction of being the oldest songs in the repertoire – having their origins deep in the roots of Irish balladry.

Fig. 1.8 – Expo '67. Ville de Montréal. Gestion de documents et archives.

Fig. 1.9 – Report of the Montreal performance in the Montreal Star, *Aug. 4, 1967.*

Fig 1.10 (Below) – The Men of the Deeps, their first recording (Apex).

Expo '67 was a wonderful experience for the group. Although no one expected to be billed as big stars, the men were treated with respect and more than willingly accepted the challenge of presenting several short concerts each day. They were all billeted at a nearby seminary. The entire experience served as an occasion for members of the choir to get to know one another. The men had the common bond of working underground, but a deep bond of a different sort developed during that week at Expo '67 – a bond that has carried over to this day.

Following the appearance at Expo, there was interest in having The Men of the Deeps perform locally and also to make a recording. (In those days it was to be a vinyl LP.)

Among the early performances were some combined presentations in Sydney with local choirs such as The Holy Angels Chorale conducted by Sister Rita Clare, CND, a well-known Cape Breton musician respected in musical circles throughout the province. Sister Rita still exerts a strong influence on the music scene in Cape Breton Island. These concert experiences bolstered the confidence of the group, and one reviewer even predicted the longevity of The Men of the Deeps with the headline "A great tradition begins."[8]

The group's chief source of funding up to this point had been the Nova Scotia Arts Council and, to a lesser extent, Moosehead Breweries. Arnie Patterson, General Manager of that Halifax-based company, had emceed the debut concerts in November 1966 and became a strong promoter of the new choir – so strong, in fact, that for a brief time the choir was advertised as "The Moosehead Men of the Deeps." In a diplomatic move, the group found it necessary to inform the well-intentioned sponsors that to identify with any commercial company would be contrary to the wishes of those whose vision created the choir.

The choir relied on a government grant and some local fundraising to meet the costs of its first recording, the planning and production of which became the responsibility of accompanist Aubrey Boone.[9] Aubrey had joined the group in the capacity of piano accompanist following the group's return from Expo '67, and it was his skills that guided the fledgling choir through the recording process. Unfortunately for the choir, soon after the completion of the recording project, Aubrey's employment required him to relocate to Halifax, and the group was faced with the reality that, if it was to continue, a new musical director would have to be found.

Fig. 1.11 – Sr. Rita Clare, ca. 1977. Photographer unknown. Reference number: 97-92-27930. Beaton Institute, Cape Breton University.

The only other musical director with whom the group had had any experience was Sister Rita Clare. Despite the intense duties demanded by her own career, she graciously stepped in to give the group encouragement by including them in a series of concerts with her own Holy Angels Chorale. When Fred Scott (assisted by accompanist George Webb) took over as director later in 1969, The Men of the Deeps were ready for their first post-Expo appearances outside of the province.[10]

Under Fred's direction – and with the assistance of founding member Jim MacLellan – the choir was granted some funding from the Nova Scotia Arts Council enabling the group to travel to Ontario and parts of Western Canada for the first time – a concert tour that bolstered confidence and earned the group many deserved accolades.

In preparation for this anticipated concert tour, spirits were bolstered considerably when, through the intercession of Al Graham at the Cape Breton Development Corporation, the group received its first travelling outfits – a move that proved to be the beginning of a long and productive relationship between the crown corporation and The Men

Fig. 1.12 – Senator Al Graham (far left) and some high-powered political friends with the Men of the Deeps, including Hon. Sheila Copps (fifth from the left), Hon. Brian Tobin (middle), Hon. David C. Dingwall (fifth from the right) and Hon. Alan Rock (third from the right).

of the Deeps. It was also the beginning of the choir's long and supportive relationship with Senator Al Graham.

Influential, too, in the relationship between The Men of the Deeps and the Cape Breton Development Corporation was Roy MacLean (one of the "original six" who formed the nucleus of the choir back in the 1960s). Roy remained a valuable singing member of The Men of the Deeps for many years while at the same time fulfilling his position as Director of Mines Planning at DEVCO – a position which enabled him to serve as a valuable liaison between the choir and the corporation. (Roy passed away on January 26, 2016.)

And, it was during this period that Ann Terry MacLellan left her career as a successful radio and television hostess and accepted a position as Director of Tourism at the Cape Breton Development Corporation – a fortuitous event for Cape Breton and for The Men of the Deeps.[11]

The Cape Breton Development Corporation (DEVCO) had been established in 1967 to begin the process of phasing out the mines in Cape Breton and to encourage the introduction of new industries to the island. However, following the Yom Kippur War and the ensuing worldwide oil crisis in 1973, world prices for petroleum began to rise sharply, leading the Trudeau Government to re-examine the original mandate of DEVCO. The decision resulted in an expansion of DEVCO coal production – a fortuitous turn of events for Cape Breton's coal miners choir. The decision was later captured in a new song by choir member Ray Holland:

The union worked to hold the jobs some said would fade away,
Looked hard for coal for many years, then DEVCO came our way.
Instead of phasing out the mines, they gave a helping hand;
We'll prove to the nation that coal is king again.[12]

The Cape Breton Development Corporation forged a favourable and supportive relationship with The Men of the Deeps which lasted until the turn of the century.

Chapter 2

"When you come back, we will be old friends"

Late in 1974, a review by the Halifax *Chronicle Herald* columnist, Basil Deakin, paid homage to a concert by The Men of the Deeps, describing the group's performance at Dalhousie Arts Centre's Rebecca Cohn Auditorium with the caption, "The sunlit voices of the men who work deep in the dark." Mr. Deakin's much-appreciated poetic caption was in stark contrast to a promotional slogan devised by Waterloo Music Company when, in the following year, the group's first book of songs with accompanying second LP recording was released: "Coal-busting songs sung by the only coal miner chorus in North America" was the slogan that promoted the group's first product with the Ontario-based distributor.[1] Yet, both captions describe a charisma that is unique to this choir and continues to be the hallmark of its performances. The choir routinely moves with ease from a boisterous rollicking song about the "government store," for example, to a poignant, sensitive lament for the miners who have lost their lives in the mines. Long-time business manager, Yogi Muise, when once asked by an interviewer to sum up his description of a performance by the choir, replied: "It's a roller coaster of emotions"; that description has been used often over the past fifty years.

Experience has confirmed that audiences warm to the "down home," friendly image portrayed by The Men when they appear on

Fig. 2.1 Promotional flyer for The Men of the Deeps *book and second recording. Waterloo Music.*

Fig. 2.2 and 2.3 – Clippings from the Cape Breton Post, 1974, *and the* Kitchener-Waterloo Record, 1975, *capture the growing intensity of the choir's activities and their audience appeal.*

stage. Of course, wearing clothes of the workplace and greeting members of the audience with "high fives" as they enter the darkened auditorium – their helmet lights splitting the darkness – aids that image. As one reviewer expressed it:

There is definitely a rough-hewn quality to their music which they perform standing, thumbs tucked in their belts looking for all the world as if they had just come off shift, got cleaned up and were ready for a pint in the local club.... The Men of the Deeps give the impression that it would make no difference to them if they were performing in Carnegie Hall or a working man's tavern.

The casual, yet professional, demeanour of the men while on stage is genuine; and that sincerity becomes even more apparent when, as is the group's common practice, the men leave the stage and mingle with the audience at the end of each concert. The years 1973 to 1977 saw the amateur group performing in an extraordinary number of venues; these were the years that shaped the image of The Men of the Deeps as a performing ensemble.

———

Midway through 1974, a significant news article published by the Canadian Press appeared in major Canadian newspapers. It was a human interest story describing an incident involving a small group of Canadian exchange students enrolled at the Peking Language Institute; they were on an educational tour of The People's Republic of China. Apparently, the group attracted a great deal of attention when they spontaneously sang some Canadian folk songs for their curious onlookers. Their rollicking rendition of "We'll Rant and We'll Roar Like True Newfoundlanders"[2] "brought down the house," according to their spokesperson. At that time, news of Canadians in China was indeed newsworthy, for Canada had only recently renewed diplomatic relations with the communist country.[3]

The story presented a possibility that warranted further exploration. If the singing of a Newfoundland folk song by a casual group of Canadian exchange students could attract that kind of attention on a Chinese street corner, how might the people of Communist China react to a group of coal miners singing songs of Canada's working-class people?

At the time the Canadian Press article appeared, The Men of the Deeps were preparing for a performance on Parliament Hill in Ottawa on Canada

Day, July 1, 1975. Hon. Allan J. MacEachen was Minister of Foreign Affairs in 1974, and, through its connections with Ann Terry MacLellan and the Cape Breton Development Corporation, the choir had become aware that the Lester B. Pearson Building in Ottawa (which housed the Department of Foreign Affairs) contained a very fine theatre facility. A plan quickly began to materialize when our Minister of Foreign Affairs agreed to provide the Lester B. Pearson Theatre as a facility for a concert by The Men of the Deeps on the day following the Canada Day appearance. Mr. MacEachen also agreed to invite foreign embassy staff members from various nations to attend the concert. This, of course, included the embassy staff of the newest country to make Ottawa its home, The People's Republic of China.

The Canada Day concert was a thrill for The Men of the Deeps. Nicholas Goldschmidt, a Canadian impresario and one of the founders of the Canadian Opera Company stepped up to oversee the choir's sound check. He was a great support for The Men of the Deeps in those early days, and many years later he would be responsible for including The Men in a major international choral festival in Toronto (see Chapter 4). That Canada Day concert on Parliament Hill, before an audience of 70,000 people remains one of the performance highlights of the choir.

The performance at the Lester B. Pearson theatre the following day was also a thrill for the group. The concert was well attended by embassy staff members from several countries – including, to the delight of the choir members, a small delegation from the Embassy of The People's Republic of China. Our Chinese friends seemed to be very moved by the concert presentation, and in a discussion following the concert they informed the group that we would certainly be welcome in their country, and that they would be honoured if our group would accept a formal invitation to visit The People's Republic of China for a three-week concert tour in November of 1975.

Fig. 2.4 – A long way from Cape Breton in so many ways.

The road to China was not easy. The invitation from the Chinese included all expenses for the three-week period during which the choir would be performing in their country – but the group still had to get there. The reality surfaced early that, as an amateur performing group, The Men of the Deeps really didn't qualify for financial assistance of that magnitude from the Canada Council; nor could the group expect, much to its disappointment, financial assistance from the Department

Fig. 2.5 – Collage of newspaper clippings chronicling the fundraising effort for the choir's proposed tour of China. Variously: Cape Breton Post, Chronicle Herald, The Expositor (Brantford, ON).

of Foreign Affairs. But it was a unique project, and the group received a great deal of encouragement from local sources, leading to the conclusion that a fundraising campaign might be well worth undertaking. To "test the waters," a couple of foundations known for their support of unique projects were contacted: The Windsor Foundation, based in Montreal, and the MacLean Foundation (Canada Packers) based in Toronto. Their generous offers of support were enough to give The Men of the Deeps the courage to attempt to raise enough funds to cover costs of travel from Canada to Beijing and back.[4]

The choir members knew right away that it was unrealistic to assume that it could raise the amount of money needed before November. To the great delight of the choir, the Chinese government was cooperative and willingly rescheduled the tour for the following June (1976). Local, provincial and national support for the project grew steadily over the next several months, boosted by complimentary editorials in several newspapers. One of the most admirable gestures came from Cape Breton mineworkers representing the island's collieries when they voted to give personal donations via the payday "check-off" system. It was an extraordinary coming together of people, and The Men of the Deeps will be ever grateful for that show of support for a project which in the end, if we are to believe the many news media reviews of the tour, proved to be a diplomatic triumph.

MP Muir Helps To Raise Money For Men Of Deeps

From The Ottawa Bureau Of The Post

OTTAWA — Bob Muir (PC-Tuesday, May 13, 1976 Sydneys) has

Windsor Foundation and $2,000 from the McLean Foundation — Mr. Muir estimated that at least $10,000 more is needed. The group is staging fund-raising concerts in Nova Scotia to

"This project of the 'M the Deeps' is, I feel, a worthwhile one and, as a f coal miner, one that is cl my heart," the veteran To said in a letter to Prime Mi Pierre Trudeau reque further assistance.

THE CHRONICLE-HERALD

Men of the Deeps awarded federal grant

OTTAWA (Staff) — The external affairs department has approved a $3,000 grant to help send a Cape Breton coal miners' chorus on a goodwill tour of Communist China.

The grant, made under the department's special public affairs projects abroad program, is the latest contribution in a fund-raising campaign being conducted by the "Men of the Deeps"

The chorus is composed of former coal ... 21

Foundation have also been promised.

Many Cape Breton businesses have also made donations ranging from $25 to ...

Some perfo during been the to Chines

The chorus part of bution to Their China dev an invitati Embassy i a performa the deeps July 1 last

Union Endorses Planned Trip

GLACE BAY union of the UM endorsed the pl Men of the Dee people's republ

The local h from the gro

...nominated to stand for election ... June wage ...ney. The delegates chairman mittee for 18th man

Cape Breton Post, Saturday, Jan. 24

THEY DESERVE SUPPORT

The singing coal

Of Deeps upport

for the Men of sed visit to the c of China is final stages. O'Donnell, ave been way as the required been still may the the y.

THE EXPOSITOR, Saturday, Feb. 14, 1976 - 15

coal-miners' choir to tour China

Y, N.S.—North Deeps have been rehearsing for their first major tour. The invitation stemmed from a concert given at the Lester B. Pearson Building, Ottawa, attended by a delegate from the Chinese Embassy.

The choir organized in 1966 in conjunction with the Miners' Folk Society of Cape Breton chose the name, Men of the Deeps, because of the location of the mines which they work beneath the bed of the Atlantic five miles off the coast of Cape Breton.

Tragedy of mine disasters through the decades are reflected in many of the ballads.

In 1891, 125 miners lost their lives in one of the collieries, at Springhill, N.S. An explosion at No. 2 Colliery, Springhill, killed 75 men, Oct. 23, 1958. Another 39 miners died in an explosion at No. 4 Colliery, Springhill, Nov. 1, 1956.

More than 200 miners were trapped in a colliery at New Waterford, in Cape Breton, in 1917 after an explosion. The death toll was 65. One of the choir's most popular ballads is The Omen. It is based on tales told by oldsters in the community that for almost two weeks before the mine disaster all the roosters in the area crowed at dusk instead of sunrise.

Many of the ballads in the choir's repertoire were contributed to a Centennial contest in 1966 organized by Nina Cohen, one of the early promoters of the miners' choir. Among the contributors were a 100-year-old woman and a 12-year-old girl. Others were in folksong collections. The entire repertoire, the first collection of miners' songs in North

Music Company in Waterloo, Ont.

"The Cape Breton miner is no ordinary man. His story has a heart beat. It should not be allowed to die," Mrs. Cohen told the choir when it was first organized in 1966. Miners were recruited for the choir through posters she had placed in washhouses where they scrubbed up after a day's work in the mines.

Some of the miner's folk songs now sung by the Men of the Deeps were found through the assistance of Dr. Helen Creighton, a folk song collector in the Maritime provinces.

The newly formed choir gave a concert at Expo 67 the following year. None had ever sung in public other than in a church choir or community variety show.

"I marvel at what Mr. O'Donnell has accomplished. A new life has opened up for

WE WILL BE OLD FRIENDS

Fig. 2.6 – Front page news. Cape Breton Post, May 12, 1976.

Fig. 2.7 – Map of China.

Fig. 2.8 – Images of Chairman Mao were everywhere.

The Men of the Deeps arrival in China was cushioned by a three-day stopover in Tokyo where the men sampled traditional Japanese cuisine, occasionally mixed in with a Japanese version of North American fast foods. The stopover served to acclimatize the group to the radical time change, but the group's stay on the twenty-second floor of the Keio Plaza Hotel didn't do much to acclimatize the men to life in Asia. Silver Donald Cameron, in a *Weekend Magazine* article documenting the group's China experience, described our hotel as a place where "the water is potable, breakfast is bacon and eggs and everyone wears a business suit."[5] If it wasn't for visits to the Asajusa Kannon Temple and a popular Geisha house (where the choir was entertained with traditional Japanese music played on traditional Japanese instruments), the men might have thought they were staying over in Montreal or Detroit.

On leaving Tokyo the entry into China was to be via Shanghai. It was an interesting flight with some notable people on board. Canadian author Pierre Berton and his publisher, Jack McClelland were travelling to The People's Republic, presumably to promote MacLelland and Stewart publications – no doubt prompted by the recent resumption of diplomatic relations between Canada and China.[6]

Shanghai was considered one of the largest cities in the world in 1976, yet it seemed that the plane carrying The Men of the Deeps (China Airlines) was the only plane on the tarmac. Exiting the plane for a light lunch and passport inspection, suitably armed soldiers escorted The Men to the terminal. Passports were collected by officials with the assurance that they would be returned before re-boarding the plane.

The central focus of the inside of the terminal building was adorned with a huge portrait of Chairman Mao Tse-tung. That was not unexpected, but it was a stern reminder that The Men of the Deeps were, indeed, now in the land of Mao. There were many young Chinese distributing passports and doing several other chores around the terminal building. Journalist Silver Donald Cameron, travelling with The Men of the Deeps as an "honourary" member of the tenor section,[7] was struck by the seriousness of the demeanor of these workers and spontaneously suggested: "Jack, why don't you have the men sing a song before we leave!"

Fig. 2.9 – Silver Donald Cameron (centre) and Jack O'Donnell (third from the left) listen attentively to their interpreter and guide.

That was all it took. The Men are often asked to "sing" when passing through airports; why should it be any different here?

The group sang "Jolly Wee Miner Men" (Silver Donald joining in on the tenor part), and it seemed a whole different world emerged. All of a sudden the atmosphere turned super friendly – with smiles and handshakes all around. The men boarded the plane with lighter hearts – relieved to know that The People's Republic of China, indeed, has a "human" face.

Upon arriving in Beijing (at that time it was still known to the West as Peking), the men were given what felt like a royal welcome. Although they were yet to learn all the names and titles of the delegation that met them, it was obvious that one person was in charge.

Zhou Rong-jin spoke in Mandarin Chinese through an interpreter: "Welcome to our country," he began. "We understand that you sang for our compatriots in Shanghai. We want you to know that we are not used to such spontaneous gestures in China!" The interpreter (who the men later got to know as Chou Song-pai) then assured the group that they were very welcome and our hosts would now escort them to the Peking Hotel – which was to be home for the next few days.

China was still a very closed country at this time. There were no fast food chains like McDonald's or Dairy Queen; there weren't even any "corner stores." It was late evening when we arrived at the Peking Hotel. Dave Watts was hungry and asked the clerk at the front desk of the hotel "where a fella might get a hamburger at this time of night?" No response.

Shortly after our arrival at the hotel, two members of the "welcoming committee" who had greeted us at the airport stopped by for a private conversation. Zhou Rong-jin spoke, again in Mandarin Chinese, through his interpreter, Chou Song-pai. Zhou Rong-jin always spoke in Chinese when the business being discussed was serious. He was not consistently present throughout the three weeks, but Chou Song-pai was to accompany the group throughout China. He and a female guide, Li Tsun-ying, who joined the group the next day, were our constant companions. Both became very good friends.

On this first evening in China, Zou Rong-jin had some serious business to discuss. It was a delicate subject because it concerned the subject of censorship.

Prior to leaving for China, the group had been asked to send a copy of its recently published book of songs which contained most of the choir's repertoire at the time – thirty-five songs in all. Not much thought had been given that gesture until that evening when it surfaced in the hands of Zou Rong-jin. Through the interpreter, Chou Song-pai, Zou explained that China today is a controlled society. Some of the songs in The Men of the Deeps' collection may not be suitable for Chinese audiences. In particular, he cautioned, it would not be appropriate to include songs about religion, courtship or any verses pertaining to "drinking" – e.g., our song "The Government Store." That simple directive excluded seven of the songs in the repertoire of twenty-five songs that had been planned for this tour.

Rather than argue the case, the delicate situation was presented to the choir members who all agreed that we had come to China to sing, and eighteen songs were more than enough to make up any concert program.

Fig. 2.10 – Opening strains of "The Government Store," from And Now the Fields are Green, *op. cit.*

The Chinese hosts assigned to accompany The Men of the Deeps throughout the tour proved to be extremely gracious and likeable. Chou Song-pai's favourite greeting to us was very touching: "Now we are friends," he would say. "When you come back, we will be old friends."

The extraordinary trust and confidence they placed in the members of the choir was evident from that very first week in Beijing. Silver Donald Cameron, in the second of his four-part series documenting the tour of China, expressed that trust succinctly when he described a very intimate moment that was meant exclusively for The Men of the Deeps as respected visitors from abroad. "In Peking, we were led into a clothing store: as dozens of shoppers looked on, our guide pressed a button and a section of the floor behind a counter slid away. A staircase took us down into a labyrinth of tunnels under the city.

"Two Pekings," explained Chou. "One on the surface, the other underground."[8] Chou song-pai went on to explain that they "can put the entire city underground in less than ten minutes, and keep the people comfortable there for weeks."[9]

Silver Donald, had been given permission to take photographs of our trip throughout the three week stay, however, for security reasons, he was asked, politely, not to photograph the underground complex. And at a banquet given for the group before leaving Peking three weeks later, officials and staff members at the Canadian Embassy informed us that they had never had the privilege of viewing Peking's "underground city." That should say something about how our Chinese hosts felt about their fellow mine workers from Canada.

When The Men left Peking they were brought to the coast – to Tienjin, a large city known for its "rug" industry. There, and in the remaining cities on the tour, we were often startled by female voices being broadcast from many street corners throughout the city – important announcements, apparently, meant for the general populace. Occasionally the guides would announce: "They are speaking about you!"

Fig. 2.11 – Weekend Magazine article (first of a series of four) by Silver Donald Cameron.

Fig. 2.12 – Tapestry display in Tienjin.

The visit to Tienjin served to introduce the group to average Chinese workers and sophisticated methods of rug making. Tienjin rugs are famous all over the world. Later on the tour, The Men visited a musical instrument factory where they observed the construction of a piano from the "raw log" stage to the final elegantly finished grand piano. These visits emphasized the concept that "ordinary workers" are the backbone of modern China's society.

The true meaning and purpose of The Men of the Deeps tour of China began to surface when they arrived in the large industrial city of Tangshan. This was the site of the group's first major concert of the tour. It was also the site of some of China's most productive coal mines.

The hotel in Tangshan was newly built, and the men were informed that they were the first foreign visitors to stay there. One of the most memorable recollections of the entire China experience came on that first day in

Tangshan, and it was vividly described in one of Silver Donald's *Weekend Magazine* stories::

> The night which lives most vibrantly in memory is that night in Tangshan when Jack and I suggested we all wander downtown after dinner and sing for the people in the streets. We asked Chou to come along to explain who we were. He gathered the other interpreters, and we set out in the twilight.
>
> Down the long, walled street to the gate of the park, and along a wide thoroughfare in the gathering darkness, curious people trailed behind us. We lined up on the concrete steps of what seemed to be a workers' club and asked Chou to explain. He shouted in Chinese, nodded, and we began. We looked out on a semicircle of bewildered, tentative faces, and launched into "The Man with the Torch in His Cap." The perplexity turned to smiles, to pleasure, to applause.
>
> We sang "Tienanmen,"[10] and the crowd laughed aloud: so funny, these Canadians who appear from nowhere and sing one of our songs in their queer, exotic language. And yet – one of our songs! Beaming approval, the crowd began clapping in rhythm.
>
> We ended, and walked on down the street. The crowd followed, perhaps four or five hundred, swelling as people came from the alleys and courtyards: there's something going on in the street. Around a corner onto an enormous avenue, 50 yards wide, perhaps more, with the Chinese pressing up against us, children grinning at us, hands shaking, knee-hah! Under a street light we stopped again, gathered on the curb, the last light fading behind the half-finished apartment block across the road, the mass of grinning, excited faces melting into the dark distances, a thousand people, fifteen hundred, willing us to sing: "And many a miner has laid his head / In death on the coal's black lap; / So don't forget he's a hero too: / The man with the torch in his cap."
>
> And again that passport to Chinese hearts, their song, "Tienanmen": "Our great leader. Chairman Mao, He leads us marching on." And suddenly it burst, that membrane of reserve which keeps strangers apart, burst, and the people of Tangshan surged into our midst and we into theirs, the distance dissolved, the barriers swept away, the language conquered. Al Provoe walked down the centre of the street with a Chinese child holding each hand, capering and squalling. Alex MacDonald shot by on a bicycle while its owner held his jacket and roared his enjoyment. Then everyone

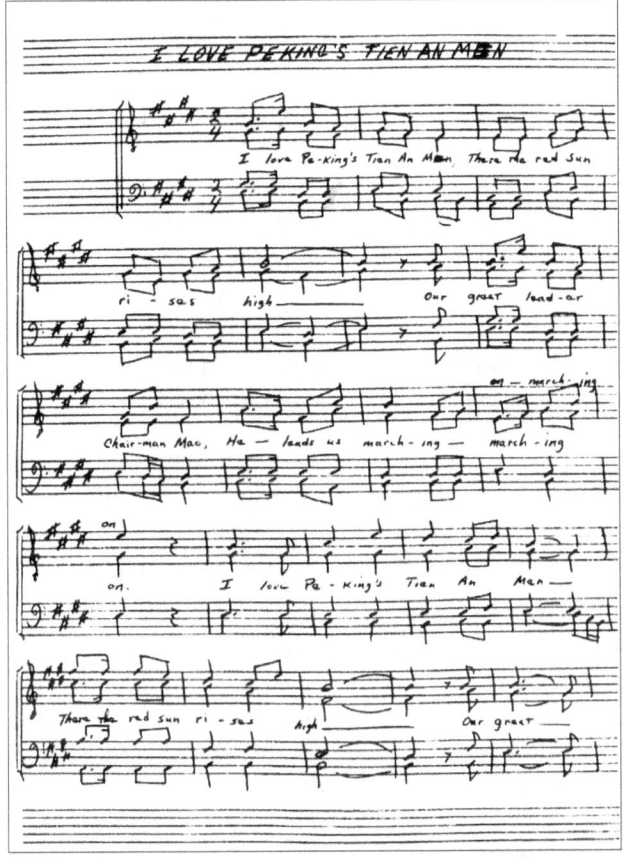

Fig. 2.13 – O'Donnell's arrangement for "I Love Peking's Tien An Min."

Figs. 2.14, 2.15 – The Men of the Deeps out for a stroll and an appreciative crowd lining the street to see them.

seemed to be on bicycles, Bob McLeod wobbling along, his first bike ride in forty years, Sid Forgeron vanishing into the dusk. Chou clutched Jack O'Donnell by the arm, telling him, "You have made that song much more beautiful. Really. Really." And Donnie Matheson walked beside me and said, in an awed whisper, "Look behind you." I looked, and as far as I could see that immense street was choked with people: mothers with baby carriages, old people, young people, children, people on bicycles, people on foot, people running, people walking, people clapping.

And here and there a tall stout figure surrounded and smiling: a Cape Breton coal miner, in the warm Chinese evening, in the warm Chinese crowd. We sang again and turned up a side street making for the hotel, the crowd thinning as we went, though a good part of it followed us right to the door. Alex MacDonald came by. "I can't find that kid," he said. "I don't know where he went." What kid? "He came up beside me," said Alex, moved almost beyond speaking, "and I saw him tugging at his jacket. I didn't know what he was doing. He was tugging away so hard, and it took him quite a while, and then he came running up and pushed this in my hand. I wanted to give him a maple leaf, but when I turned around he was gone." He held out his hand.

In it was a tiny metal badge – a merit badge of the Young Communists, someone said later, a thing so precious the boy should never have given it away. "I don't know what it is," said Alex. "But I'll tell you, b'y, I'll treasure that little jigger for the rest of me life."

The concert performance the following night was exhilarating. The group didn't have to worry that no one in the audience understood English; as became the custom throughout the tour, to accommodate the audience, Chou Song-pai translated the explanations about our group and the music.

We were catapulted into another "high" following the concert, and when we returned to the hotel, no one was ready to retire for the evening. As is often the situation at home, some of the choir members brought their guitars (and voices) to the lobby for a little celebration. It was, after all the "birthday week" for both Bob MacLeod and Jack O'Donnell.

Although "a good time was had by all," apparently the men had overstepped their bounds when they welcomed the young staff members at the hotel to join in. The next morning Zou Rong-Jin appeared with a polite reprimand: Again in Chinese Mandarin, he cautioned that "In China, we do not celebrate birthdays!"

Perhaps one of the highlights of the entire tour occurred in Tangshan when The Men of the Deeps were invited to join a group of Chinese miners in a tour of an underground mine. "We crowded into the cage like commuters on a subway," wrote Silver Donald Cameron, "elbows snug to our sides, pit helmets clacking together, a mass of blue-clad Chinese and Canadians, miners, guides and officials. With a hardly perceptible jerk the cage dropped towards the mine roads 1,300 feet below....

Down deep in a coal mine, underneath the ground
Where a gleam of sunshine never can be found.
Digging dusky diamonds, all the seasons road.
Down Deep in a coal mine underneath the ground.

The mine officials and the handful of Canadians who had stayed on the surface heard it floating up from the mine shaft, softer and softer as the cage dropped, four-part harmony, a driving, cheerful sound."[11] And as the cage came to a stop, Ike Lambert was heard to say: "We're half way home!"

Throughout the tour it became apparent that a unique bond was developing between the members of the choir, their guides and the array of hosts that accompanied them into factories, enjoyed their concerts – both planned and spontaneous – and feted them with entertainment and sumptuous Chinese meals. And, too, the philosophical rhetoric stressing the trials, hardships and intricacies of the Chinese revolution which brought Mao Tse-tung's country to its present state became comfortably familiar to the members of the choir, and nurtured a respect that deepened throughout the tour.

That visit to the mine in Tangshan had done much to strengthen the bond between these miners from opposite sides of the globe, and when the men learned two weeks later, following their return to Canada, that the city of Tangshan had been devastated by two major earthquakes, choir members were stunned. At last count, more than 255,000 people had lost their lives (although many experts estimate that the final death toll was two to three times that number). With warm memories of the many friends they had made on their recent visit to that very area, a message of concern and condolence was promptly sent to the region via the Canadian Embassy in Peking. Partially influenced by some of the rhetoric heard from the Chinese hosts throughout the tour, the message read: "Be assured that the thoughts of The Men of the Deeps and all the coal miners of Cape Breton are with you in these difficult times. We have great confidence that the Chinese people, who have overcome great hardships in the past, will, in the spirit of

Fig. 2.16 – cartoon by Redmond Curtis.

self-reliance and self-determination for which they are well known, recover from their unfortunate tragedy."12

A poignant moment happened while the group was visiting Shenyang, the largest city in China's industrial northeast. It was June 11, known as Davis Day back home, and a public holiday in industrial Cape Breton, named for Bill Davis, a coal miner who was shot by coal company police during the great strike of 1925. The Chinese had insisted that The Men of the Deeps not include hymns in the concert repertoire while in China. During that first evening in Shenyang, however, it was time for a rehearsal, and in the seclusion of a hotel room the men took that opportunity to sing their tribute to all miners who have lost their lives in the mines: "The Miners' Memorial Hymn":

> Go. labour on beneath the earth,
>
> In tombs that are devoid of light;
>
> Where those who perished found rebirth
>
> Their lamps eternity to light.13

How ironic, as Silver Donald Cameron observed in one of his *Weekend Magazine* articles, that "at the moment when The Men of the Deeps probably felt closest to the experiences and ideas out of which the Chinese revolution developed, they should be obliged to retreat to a private room to sing out their feelings in a hymn."14

Shenyang provided an opportunity for another heart-warming concert; and, as was the custom in most cities, the men were also entertained by Chinese performers. Surprisingly, in the Shenyang audience the men found themselves in the company of a touring group from Newfoundland. That encounter in Shenyang, with the exception of the people they were to meet later at the Canadian Embassy, was the group's only encounter with other Westerners.

Fig. 2.17 – Opening refrain of "Miner's Memorial Hymn," From And Now the Fields are Green, *op. cit.*

The business manager of The Men of the Deeps at the time was Reg Lambert, an outstanding soloist and a dedicated choir member. Reg had helped with organizing many of the minor details that go along with a trip of this nature; he, along with treasurer, Gordon Sheriff, who had managed many of the financial intricacies of the tour, were important components to the success of the Chinese venture. Reg had not been feeling well, and in Shenyang it became evident that he needed medical attention. He was admitted to hospital, and Bob Roper, willing to sacrifice his visit to Fushun, stayed in Shenyang with him while the rest of the group continued .

It was evident that someone was needed to carry on with Reg's duties as business manager. In a hastily planned meeting, Yogi Muise was elected by the group to take on the duties of business manager – a position which he continued to hold for the next thirty-three years. Reg's illness was a major concern for the choir members, and at one point there was a question as to whether or not he would be well enough to travel back to North America with the group. Our fears were eventually allayed when medical approval for him to travel was given by the time we returned to Peking.

The highlight of the group's visit to Fushun was an extensive tour of one of the world's largest open pit mines. Known as the Magnificent West Pit, the mine has been in operation since about the 12th century. Fushun was originally known as "City of Coal" and throughout its long history, the group was informed, many practical industrial cost-saving features have emanated from Fushun. Choir members were impressed, for example, when they learned that dangerous methane gas, which is pumped out of the coal mines to minimize the risk of an explosion, provides fuel for the city's stoves and furnaces. This made a lasting impression on the group. "We could be doing that," said Tommy Tighe, "but we just waste it. These people don't waste anything."[15]

Fig. 2.18, 2.19 – (Above and left) views of the tramway into the open pit mine at Funshun. Photo by Gordon Sheriff.

Back in Peking, following a trip to the Great Wall, we were feted by our hosts at a banquet at the Summer Palace, an impressive monument featuring an elegant promenade winding along an artificial lake – and home to a huge barge known as the "Marble Boat."[16] Following a sumptuous meal topped off with a serving of moth larvae soup, the group enjoyed a boat ride (not on the marble boat – which is permanently moored and sitting at the edge of the lake). It seemed appropriate to break into song, so the men began the familiar round, "Row, row, row your boat gently up

Fig. 2.20 – Jack O'Donnell holds onto the PRC flag, and to his straw hat, during a boat ride.

the stream." It wasn't long before our guides cautioned us that, "in China, we would sing: Row, row, row your boat **vigourously up the stream!**"

Silver Donald recalls that on that same day there was another group of foreigners sailing on the lake. They were somewhat of a rollicking, boisterous crowd whose singing of "The International" in French could be heard floating over the glistening lake waters. Silver Donald pegged them as "lefties" from France making an attempt to impress their Chinese hosts with their left wing view of life.

The visit to the Great Wall was, of course, a particular high point of the three-week visit to The People's Republic of China. Anticipating the trip home, choir members impressed their guides and other onlookers with a stirring patriotic rendition of "O Canada." Patriotism was an emotion that the Chinese people understood. A variety of gifts and tokens had been presented to The Men of the Deeps throughout the tour, but perhaps the most meaningful and memorable gift was an original drawing of a conversation between Chairman Mao and Dr. Norman Bethune, the Canadian physician who is effectively credited with bringing modern medicine to rural China (see figure 2.24). Although his mission in China was to support Mao's forces, he is remembered for his treatment of sick villagers as much as wounded soldiers. His selfless commitment to the Chinese people made such an impression on Chairman Mao (there are different English spellings of Mao's name) that generations of Chinese students were required to memorize the Chairman's eulogy to him. Following the choir's return from China, the work of art was presented at a ceremony to Dan Munroe, Mayor of Glace Bay. It now hangs in The Men of the Deeps Theatre at Glace Bay's Cape Breton Miners' Museum.[17]

The tour ended with a generous banquet given by the staff at the Canadian Embassy who informed the men that, from the embassy's perspective, the tour was unprecedented because The Men of the Deeps did not come on official business. Silver Donald Cameron summed it up this way:

> "...with the miners' music and laughter, their jokes and their audacity, their utter lack of snobbery – who else would sing for the kitchen staff in every hotel along the way? – they touched the Chinese in a way foreigners rarely manage, they made friends for Canada among people who scarcely know where the country is located."

The Men of the Deeps departed China with a renewed faith in humanity and with a strong feeling of confidence in their mission to champion songs of the working people. All were moved when Chou Song-pai bid The Men farewell with his favourite: "Now we are friends; when you come back we will be old friends."

(Clockwise from top left)
Fig. 2.21 – An impromptu chorus of "O Canada" in front of the Great Wall.

Fig. 2.22 – The Great Wall. Photo by Gordon Sheriff.

Fig. 2.23 – Jack O'Donnell. Photo by Gordon Sheriff.

Fig. 2.24 – Portrait of Chairman Mao and Dr. Norman Bethune. Photo by Gordon Sheriff.

Fig. 2.25 – Images of Chairman Mao were everywhere. Photo by Gordon Sheriff.

Fig. 2.26 – A few of The Men in front of a friendship billboard. Photo by Gordon Sheriff.

WE WILL BE OLD FRIENDS

Chapter 3

"The authentic voices of Nova Scotia"

"No songs about God, love or booze for Canadian miners in China" was the headline that greeted The Men of the Deeps when they arrived in Vancouver en route home from the historic tour of The People's Republic of China. At the Canadian Embassy banquet given for the choir before departing from Beijing, a prominent Canadian journalist had been present: Ross Munro, in the mid 1970s, was bureau chief in Beijing for the *Globe and Mail.* And, in 1978 he also became *Time* magazine's bureau chief in Bangkok, New Delhi and Hong Kong where he continued to build on his reputation as one of North America's major correspondents on Asian affairs.

Mr. Munro had followed the progress of The Men of the Deeps tour closely and was particularly curious about the censorship issue that challenged the men upon their arrival in China. Having been informed that the group was requested to omit songs about religion, courtship and drinking from the repertoire, he asked, "Why was the group allowed to sing that song about Big Flora?"

He was referring to one of the original songs that had come to The Men of the Deeps via the song-writing contest that preceded the founding of the group. The song is actually "Kelly's Cove," a Cape Breton version of "Blackleg Miners," a British folk song about scab labour.

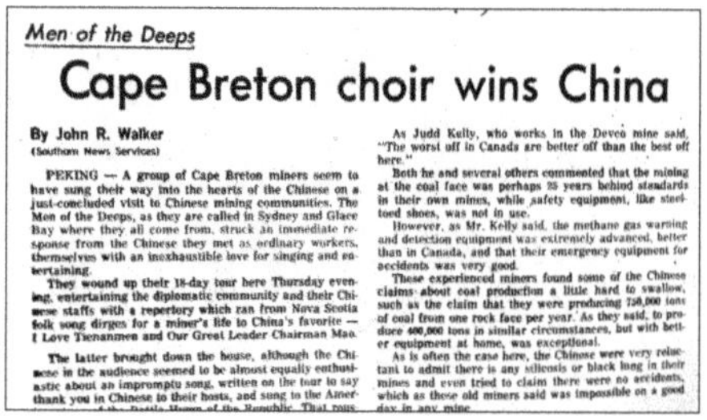
Men of the Deeps

Cape Breton choir wins China

By John R. Walker
(Southam News Services)

PEKING — A group of Cape Breton miners seem to have sung their way into the hearts of the Chinese on a just-concluded visit to Chinese mining communities. The Men of the Deeps, as they are called in Sydney and Glace Bay where they all come from, struck an immediate response from the Chinese they met as ordinary workers, themselves with an inexhaustible love for singing and entertaining.

They wound up their 18-day tour here Thursday evening, entertaining the diplomatic community and their Chinese staffs with a repertory which ran from Nova Scotia folk song dirges for a miner's life to China's favorite — I Love Tienanmen and Our Great Leader Chairman Mao.

The latter brought down the house, although the Chinese in the audience seemed to be almost equally enthusiastic about an impromptu song, written on the tour to say thank you in Chinese to their hosts, and sung to the Amer-

As Judd Kelly, who works in the Devco mine said, "The worst off in Canada are better off than the best off here."

Both he and several others commented that the mining at the coal face was perhaps 25 years behind standards in their own mines, while safety equipment, like steel-toed shoes, was not in use.

However, as Mr. Kelly said, the methane gas warning and detection equipment was extremely advanced, better than in Canada, and that their emergency equipment for accidents was very good.

These experienced miners found some of the Chinese claims about coal production a little hard to swallow, such as the claim that they were producing 750,000 tons of coal from one rock face per year. As they said, to produce 400,000 tons in similar circumstances, but with better equipment at home, was exceptional.

As is often the case here, the Chinese were very reluctant to admit there is any silicosis or black lung in their mines and even tried to claim there were no accidents, which as these old miners said was impossible on a good

Fig. 3.1 – Newspaper clipping, unknown source.

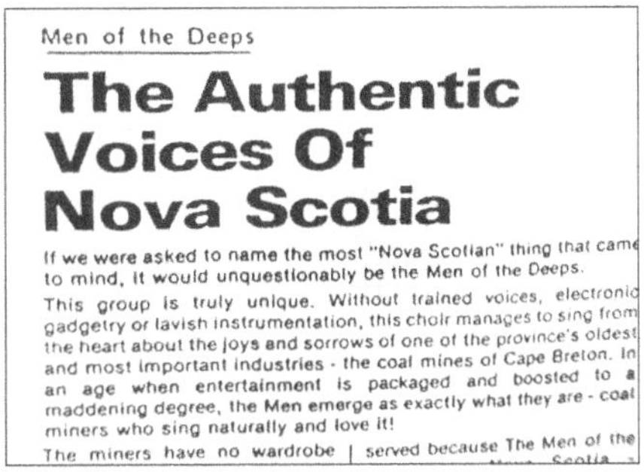
Men of the Deeps

The Authentic Voices Of Nova Scotia

If we were asked to name the most "Nova Scotian" thing that came to mind, it would unquestionably be the Men of the Deeps.

This group is truly unique. Without trained voices, electronic gadgetry or lavish instrumentation, this choir manages to sing from the heart about the joys and sorrows of one of the province's oldest and most important industries - the coal mines of Cape Breton. In an age when entertainment is packaged and boosted to a maddening degree, the Men emerge as exactly what they are - coal miners who sing naturally and love it!

The miners have no wardrobe | served because The Men of the

Fig. 3.2 – Copy of Antigonish Casket *article (n.d.) reprinted in DEVCO newsletter (n.d.).*

The Cape Breton adaptation mocks seasonal workers imported from the United States to the New Campbellton mine operation at the base of Kelly's Mountain in the late 1800s. The Cape Breton variant has a verse which makes reference to a popular drop-in place for the unwelcome migrant workers: "Big Flora keeps a hall where the miners always call, when they're coming in the fall...." When the song was explained to him, Mr. Munro apparently concluded that the Chinese censors overlooked what could have been read into that verse and allowed the song, with its rousing chorus, a rallying cry for miners to join their union: "Join the union or you'll die, Join the union or you'll die ... among the Yappie (i.e., Yankee) miners!"

Before leaving the banquet and reception that evening, Ross Munro assured the group that his press release would centre on the many positive aspects of the concert tour. And he did, indeed, write a very heart-warming, genuine account extolling the many positive interactions between the coal miners from Canada's Cape Breton Island and their fellow workers on the other side of the globe. Unfortunately, however, Mr. Munro had no say in the wording of the headlines which various newspapers would choose to introduce the story. The *Globe and Mail* chose to adorn its front page with the headline "No songs about God, love or booze for Canadian miners in China." But, perhaps in an effort to catch the attention of more readers, the *Globe and Mail* went one step further by adding a sub-headline which read: "Big Flora slips by Peking officials!"

And even though the Ottawa *Journal* in our nation's capitol generously concluded Ross Munro's story with the assertion that The Men of the Deeps tour of The People's Republic of China was "the best people-to-people exchange ever between two countries," that newspaper nevertheless could not resist headlining the story with the caption: "Coal canaries gagged."

—

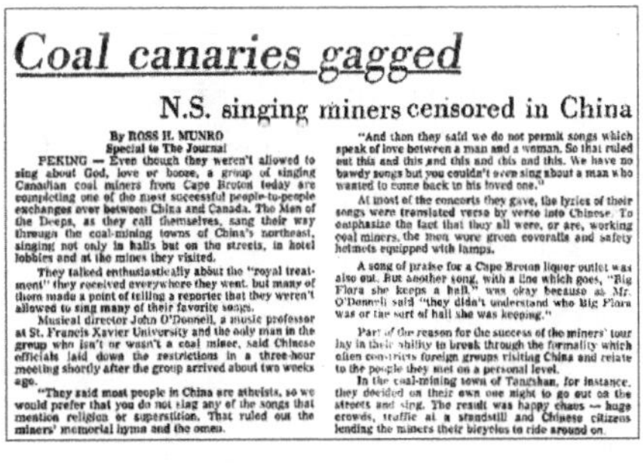
Coal canaries gagged

N.S. singing miners censored in China

By ROSS H. MUNRO
Special to The Journal

PEKING — Even though they weren't allowed to sing about God, love or booze, a group of singing Canadian coal miners from Cape Breton today are completing one of the most successful people-to-people exchanges ever between China and Canada. The Men of the Deeps, as they call themselves, sang their way through the coal-mining towns of China's northeast, singing not only in halls but on the streets, in hotel lobbies and at the mines they visited.

They talked enthusiastically about the "royal treatment" they received everywhere they went, but many of them made a point of telling a reporter that they weren't allowed to sing many of their favorite songs.

Musical director John O'Donnell, a music professor at St. Francis Xavier University and the only man in the group who isn't or wasn't a coal miner, said Chinese officials laid down the restrictions in a three-hour meeting shortly after the group arrived about two weeks ago.

"They said most people in China are atheists, so we would prefer that you do not sing any of the songs that mention religion or superstition. That ruled out the miners' memorial hymn and the amen.

"And then they said we do not permit songs which speak of love between a man and a woman. So that ruled out this and this and this and this and this. We have no bawdy songs but you couldn't even sing about a man who wanted to come back to his loved one."

At most of the concerts they gave, the lyrics of their songs were translated verse by verse into Chinese. To emphasize the fact that they all were, or are, working coal miners, the men wore green coveralls and safety helmets equipped with lamps.

A song of praise for a Cape Breton liquor outlet was also out. But another song, with a line which goes, "Big Flora she keeps a hall," was okay because as Mr. O'Donnell said "they didn't understand who Big Flora was or the sort of hall she was keeping."

Part of the reason for the success of the miners' tour lay in their ability to break through the formality which often constricts foreign groups visiting China and relate to the people they met on a personal level.

In the coal-mining town of Tangshan, for instance, they decided on their own one night to go out on the streets and sing. The result was happy chaos — huge crowds, traffic at a standstill and Chinese citizens lending the miners their bicycles to ride around on.

Fig. 3.3 – Ottawa Journal, *June 1976.*

The return trip home from Vancouver to Cape Breton should have been uneventful. It wasn't!

A pre-arranged concert performance one day after arriving in Vancouver went very well, but the planned departure for the East Coast the next day did not! The group awoke the next morning to the news that Air Canada was embroiled in a major strike. It was a bit of a nightmare for The Men of the Deeps whose members had anticipated an enthusiastic welcoming from family and friends back home in Cape Breton. Expecting the strike to be resolved in a day or two, the men waited in anticipation, biding their time on the campus of the University of British Columbia.

After a week with no resolution to the strike in sight, the men set off by bus to Seattle to book whatever flights might be available to get them back to the East Coast. Much of the burden of booking new flights fell to our newly elected business manager, Yogi Muise. With newspaper photos and stories of our successful tour of China in hand, he was able to persuade booking agents at the Seattle-Tacoma Airport to streamline a route across the United States.

The return flights took the group via Chicago's O'Hare Airport to Boston's Logan Airport where hotel accommodations were waiting. The group arrived in Bangor, Maine, the following day, and, again with photos and news stories in hand, plus some assurance from Ann Terry MacLellan at DEVCO that these unexpected expenses would be covered, our business manager was able to rent a bus to traverse the remainder of the trip home.

All of this had gone relatively smoothly – until the rented bus broke down on Maine's Route 9 (often referred to as the Airline Highway). This was not the trip home that the men had anticipated. Another bus was, of course, provided – but only after a two-and-a-half-hour wait sitting on the side of the highway.

Things became even more complicated when the bus arrived at the Canadian border between Calais, Maine, and St. Stephen, New Brunswick. Although the group had gone through a rather thorough customs check upon arrival in Vancouver, the customs officials at the Maine/New Brunswick border insisted that the bus be emptied and that all luggage made available for a thorough inspection (a decision which might have been arrived at when the customs officials learned that these men were actually on their way back from The People's Republic of China!)

When the trip finally resumed, the men broke into song as the bus trundled along the highways toward their beloved Cape Breton.

It was in the wee hours of the next morning when the group finally arrived in Sydney (having dropped off their conductor in Antigonish three hours earlier). There were no balloons or flags to welcome The Men of the Deeps home – just the warmth and enthusiasm of their loved ones who had been waiting patiently for that special moment.

—

There was not much time to savour the warmth of family and friends. The Men of the Deeps had been booked to perform at the upcoming 1976 Summer Olympics in Montreal in July – a highlight of which was an interview by American broadcaster, Pierre Salinger, aired south of the border on National Public Radio. In the early 1960s Mr. Salinger had achieved notoriety as White House Press Secretary to John F. Kennedy and Lyndon B. Johnson; he was also campaign manager for Robert Kennedy's bid for the presidency of the United States. He returned to a career in journalism following the Kennedy/Johnson era, and The Men of the Deeps were fortunate to have attracted enough of his attention to warrant a special interview at those Montreal Olympic celebrations. This broadcast on National Public Radio was the first introduction of The Men of the Deeps to a widespread audience south of the border.

Montréal 1976

Fig. 3.4 – '76 Olympics logo.

Upon returning once again to Nova Scotia, the group went on to perform at the Atlantic Folk Festival in August and, in September, the United Mine Workers of America brought Cape Breton's singing miners to Cincinnati, Ohio, to perform for its annual international convention. A formal appearance in December on the popular night time television talk show, *Ninety Minutes Live* with Peter Gzowski, concluded the group's 1976 performance commitments.[1]

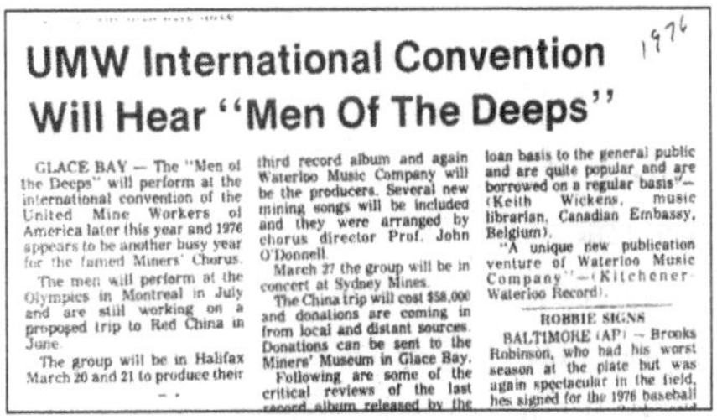

UMW International Convention Will Hear "Men Of The Deeps"

1976

GLACE BAY — The "Men of the Deeps" will perform at the international convention of the United Mine Workers of America later this year and 1976 appears to be another busy year for the famed Miners' Chorus.

The men will perform at the Olympics in Montreal in July and are still working on a proposed trip to Red China in June.

The group will be in Halifax March 20 and 21 to produce their third record album and again Waterloo Music Company will be the producers. Several new mining songs will be included and they were arranged by chorus director Prof. John O'Donnell.

March 27 the group will be in concert at Sydney Mines.

The China trip will cost $58,000 and donations are coming in from local and distant sources. Donations can be sent to the Miners' Museum in Glace Bay.

Following are some of the critical reviews of the last record album released by the ... loan basis to the general public and are quite popular and are borrowed on a regular basis" — (Keith Wickens, music librarian, Canadian Embassy, Belgium).

"A unique new publication venture of Waterloo Music Company" — (Kitchener-Waterloo Record).

ROBBIE SIGNS

BALTIMORE (AP) — Brooks Robinson, who had his worst season at the plate but was again spectacular in the field, has signed for the 1976 baseball

Fig. 3.5 – Newspaper clipping. Source unknown.

A fitting closure to the entire China experience came early in 1977 when The Men of the Deeps received an invitation from the Canadian Broadcasting Corporation to appear on the popular weekly television show *Front Page Challenge.*

The appearance on *Front Page Challenge* was truly the "frosting on the cake" event of the entire China experience. The group was brought to Halifax for the taping of the show. The very nature of the story required that The Men of the Deeps be "hidden challengers" – i.e., the men were not to be seen by the panel either before or during the show. Consequently, it was a requirement that the group be sequestered in a school classroom until show time.

In order to maintain that confidentiality, all the choir members (with the exception of the conductor and one singer) were ushered into the auditorium just prior to the opening of the doors to the public. The men were seated in aisle seats throughout the auditorium – dressed in ordinary street clothes, but with their mining helmets hidden discreetly under each seat. At the appropriate time during the show, Jack O'Donnell and Bobby Roper (Bobby, dressed as The Men of the Deeps usually appear in concert, in mining coveralls and mining helmet mounted with pit lamp) took their place behind the panel members; they could only be seen by the narrator, Fred Davis, and of course by the audience.

The panel members were long-time staples of the popular television show: Gordon Sinclair, Pierre Berton and Betty Kennedy; the invited guest panelist for that week was Gerald Regan – at that time, Premier of Nova Scotia. After several failures by the regular panel members to identify the story, it was Premier Regan who eventually came up with the correct answer when he interrupted panelist Pierre Berton to exclaim: "These are the Cape Breton coal miners, The Men of the Deeps, who travelled to China last summer!"

That's when the fun began! Fred Davis gestured toward the audience and informed the panel members that not only did they have the conductor and one of the singers here, but the entire choir was here to entertain and answer questions. That, of course, was the cue for the choir members to don their pit helmets (pit lamps turned on) and make their way through the darkened auditorium and onto the stage.

The round of questioning from the panel members was delightful and informative. Fred Davis first acknowledged Ann Terry MacLellan who, in her role with the Cape Breton Development Corporation, had arranged for the necessary "time off" to allow the group to appear on *Front Page Challenge*. (Terry had often been a guest panelist on the popular show.) He then turned the questioning over to the panel members who singled out several individual members to recall their experiences of China. And, of course, the men were invited to sing for the audience as the show concluded with the running of credits.

Front Page Challenge always featured two stories for its panelists to challenge. The companion story for the program on which The Men of the Deeps appeared was about the recent decision of the Canadian government to establish the 200-mile fishing zone – a decision that was hugely popular with Atlantic fishermen. The guest challenger for that story was, of course, the Honorable Romeo LeBlanc, Minister of Fisheries and Oceans in the cabinet of Prime Minister Pierre Elliott Trudeau.

In a very special way, the decision to combine the story of the extended fishing zone with the story of The Men of the Deeps in China was timely and appropriate, for it was while the men were touring China that, on the other side of the world, the decision to extend Canada's fishing rights was publicly announced. Recalling that day in China, Silver Donald Cameron recorded an interesting conversation he had had with Chou Song-pai while the choir was en route from one venue to another: "One morning he boarded the bus and slipped into the seat beside me" wrote Silver Donald. "This morning on the radio, some news from Canada. Apparently your government has declared an extension of territorial waters."[2] This subject particularly interested Chou Song-pai and he was anxious to test the opinions of this well-read "tenor" travelling with the group. Silver Donald skillfully wove many of those conversations with our Chinese guides throughout his *Weekend Magazine* articles documenting the China experience.

Perhaps it was no coincidence that the producers of CBC's *Front Page Challenge* chose to combine the story of Canada's decision to extend its fishing rights with the story of the Cape Breton's singing coal miners' diplomatic success in the People's Republic of China.

—

The remaining years of the decade didn't provide much downtime for The Men of the Deeps. The choir's many performances at the Miners' Museum in Glace Bay and at several venues throughout the province prompted one reviewer to dub them "The authentic voices of Nova Scotia."[3] Unique among the engagements of the closing years of the 1970s were the concerts presented for passengers on Cape Breton's popular, but short-lived, summer tourist attraction, the Sydney-Louisbourg Railway. Those S & L Railway performances were a treat for the choir, but apparently the tourist attraction was not lucrative enough to maintain it for more than a couple of years.

It was in 1978 that The Men of the Deeps received an invitation from Col. Ian Fraser to perform at the inaugural Nova Scotia Military Tattoo which Fraser produced and directed to mark the first International Gathering of the Clans outside Scotland. The event, held in the summer of 1979, was attended and opened by Her Majesty Queen Elizabeth, The Queen Mother, and although the performance of the choir was somewhat dwarfed by the magnitude of the large and dynamic performances of the many visiting instrumental and military gymnastic entertainers, the choir was charmed to be granted a special personal encounter with Her Majesty following the performance.[4]

Fig. 3.6 – Royal Nova Scotia International Tattoo logo.

The Tattoo's popularity and success throughout the years warranted the granting of Royal Status by Her Majesty the Queen in 2006, a tribute to the dedication and hard work of Col. Fraser whose influence on the annual presentation can still be seen. Now known as the Royal Nova Scotia International Tattoo, it is promoted as the world's largest annual indoor show.

The decade of the 1970s was good to The Men of the Deeps but not without its downside. On February 24, 1979, at approximately 4:20 a.m. an explosion occurred in Glace Bay's No. 26 colliery. Long-term choir member, Jim MacLellan, on extended leave from the choir, was Mine Manager at No. 26 at the time and was intimately involved with all who were affected by the disaster.[5] The explosion claimed ten lives underground; two others died later in a Halifax hospital. Jim will tell you that one of the most difficult moments for him following his return to the choir in 1986 was the realization that the choir's repertoire now included an arrangement of Allister MacGillivray's

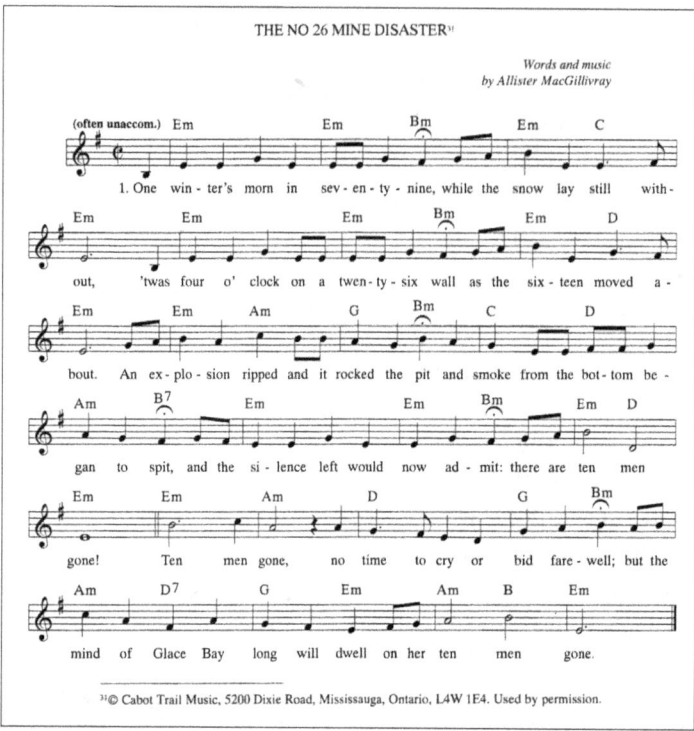

Fig. 3.7 – Partial score of "The No. 26 Mine Disaster." From And Now the Fields are Green, op. cit.

Fig. 3.8 – Davis Memorial, New Waterford, 1998. Photograph by Paul Prendergast. Reference number: 98-666-29453. Beaton Institute, Cape Breton University.

haunting ballad recalling the event, "The No. 26 Mine Disaster."

And in that same year, on July 9, Alan Tighe, the son of long-time choir member Tommy Tighe, was killed in a mine accident at Lingan Colliery in New Waterford. Alan was the nephew of Eddie Tighe, also a faithful member of The Men of the Deeps. The Tighe brothers have both since passed away, but choir members still recall with affection their long-term commitment to the choir.

Earlier in the decade, on March 3, 1973, the body of New Waterford miner, Earl Leadbeater, was never recovered following a fire at No. 12 Colliery.[6] The mine was eventually sealed off and a commemorative stone marks the final resting place of the New Waterford miner. Mining engineer, Donald MacFadgen, was also a fatality of that accident, suffering a fatal heart attack while combating the fire in the mine. The mine was lost, and the grounds above No. 12 Colliery in New Waterford have been converted to a park commemorating all Cape Breton miners who have perished in the mines. An array of flags adorning the park serves to honour the multiplicity of immigrant workers who arrived on the shores of Cape Breton to work in the mines of the coal-rich island.

The international United Mine Workers of America has been a constant supporter of The Men of the Deeps since the group first appeared in public in 1966. This was initially revealed in the strong role played by the UMWA at the opening of the Miners' Museum in Glace Bay in 1967. Throughout the years, the international organization has

displayed that loyalty to the group in various ways, but most particularly at the Davis Day ceremonies held annually in the various communities which make up industrial Cape Breton. In 1976, as previously noted, the choir performed at the organization's international convention in Cincinnati, Ohio. It was a tribute to the choir when, in December 1979, the group was again invited to perform for the UMWA annual convention in Denver, Colorado – a fitting end to the decade.

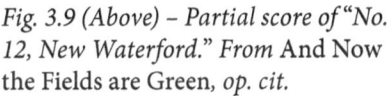

Fig. 3.9 (Above) – Partial score of "No. 12, New Waterford." From And Now the Fields are Green, *op. cit.*

Fig. 3.10 – Newspaper clipping. Source unknown.

Chapter 4

They expose their souls

> Their code of life has passed the test of time,
> through their music they expose their souls.[1]

The decades of the 1980s and 1990s challenged the time and talents of The Men of the Deeps to heights that not even the enthusiastic and visionary minds that gave birth to the group could have imagined. The popularity of the choir expanded considerably throughout this period. No one was more surprised than the men themselves when a reference to the choir suddenly surfaced on the popular American television program, *Jeopardy*. The category was "Canada," the clue was "The Men of the Deeps," and the answer (put in the form of a question) was "What are coal miners?"

The rapid rise in performance commitments throughout the late 1970s and into the 1980s had brought with it a realization that there was more to these commitments than signing contracts and boarding buses and planes; there was the ever-expanding need for new and original repertoire that needed some attention. There was, of course, the small collection of songs remaining from the 1967 song writing contest that had been organized by Nina Cohen and Dr. Helen Creighton. Songs like "Kelly's Cove," "Little Pinkie Engine," "The Omen" and "The Man With a Torch in His Cap"; those had become part of the choir's standard repertoire. Helen Creighton remained faithful to her commitment to bring relevant songs to the attention of the group, and it was during this period that the influence of some of Cape Breton's past and present poets and songwriters began to surface. The music of well-loved Cape Breton bards like Charlie MacKinnon and John

Allan Cameron, past and present poets and songwriters like Lillian Crewe Walsh, Leon Dubinsky and Allister MacGillivray provided new material to bolster the choir's concert repertoire promoting the music and traditions of Cape Breton's coal mining communities.

The active participation of the choir's musical director in the Canadian Folk Music Society[2] contributed considerably to expanding the knowledge and repertoire of coal mining communities, not only of Cape Breton, but of similar communities around the world. Songs from the collections of Ontario's Edith Fowke[3] (whose publications on labour and industrial protest songs exerted a strong influence on the repertoire of the choir), British Columbia's Phil Thomas ("Are You from Bevan?"[4]) and Pennsylvania's George Korson ("We're All Jolly Wee Miner Men"[5]) began to find their way into the permanent repertoire and contributing to the historical knowledge that shaped a concert by The Men of the Deeps.

Fig. 4.1 – Partial score of "The Man With a Torch in His Cap." From *And Now the Fields are Green*, op. cit.

Others who exerted some influence on the direction the repertoire of Nova Scotia's coal miners choir was taking included Real Benoit (a singing miner from the Rouyn-Noranda area of Quebec, whose songs reveal much about the camaraderie that binds miners), and Kate Braid (a carpenter, teacher and award-winning poet from British Columbia whose relationship with The Men of the Deeps produced a touching and revealing documentary on the choir which aired on Lister Sinclair's popular CBC radio program *Ideas*); Geoff Drake, an immigrant from Wales whose passion and interest in the songs of the land of his birth, left a poignant imprint on the music of the choir, and the music of England's Northumbrian coal mining communities began to exert an influence on the choir's music when the director was introduced to Johnny Handel ("Dust in the Air"), arguably one of Northumbria's most prolific bards.

The influence from the mining areas of northern England continued into the new millennium when first tenor Nipper MacLeod had the privilege of participating in a conference at Northumbria University focusing

Fig. 4.2 – Miner and choir member Nipper MacLeod. Photo by Owen Fitzgerald.

on the issues that grew out of the famous miners' strike of 1984 in England. Accompanied by Dalhousie University researchers Drs. Judy and Larry Haiven, with support from several labour unions and funding from the Nova Scotia Department of Tourism, the conference afforded Nipper an opportunity to join in concert with one of that area's national treasures, pop singer Billy Bragg at a major fundraising gala in the historic city of Durham.

As the years progressed, the music of gifted composers and folk music enthusiasts from other countries found a place in the on-going repertoire of Cape Breton's coal miners choir: Scotland's Ian Campbell ("The Canny Miner Lad"); Ireland's Brendan Graham ("You Raise Me Up"); England's Dave Webber ("Working at the Coal Face"); and Kay Sutcliffe ("Coal, Not Dole"); Belgium's Willy Appermont and Roger Gaspercic ("No More Coal"); and from the United States the choir successfully adopted the music of Guy Clark and Roger Murrah ("Immigrant Eyes"). In recent years the music of international composer and performer, Elton John, found its way into the choir's repertoire ("Once We Were Kings"). Informative notes on all the songs in the repertoire of The Men of the Deeps are provided in appendix 4.

—

Late in 1980, the men were introduced to Canada's north when they flew to Labrador and northern Quebec on a private plane supplied by Iron-Ore Canada. For the most part, the weather in Labrador was good to the group; however, poor weather kept Brian Mulroney (then president of Iron-Ore Canada) from attending the final concert and reception in Schefferville, Quebec.

Fig. 4.3 – The Aurora, weekly newspaper serving Labrador West.

Fig. 4.4 – Newspaper clipping. Source unknown.

Preparations began early for what was to become The Men of the Deeps biggest television experience to date, the *Anne Murray Christmas Special*, later televised to audiences throughout North America. The show, which also featured famed country singer, Kris Kristofferson, was aired in December 1981. It amounted to a quasi-holiday for members of the choir – culminating in a two-week taping period divided between two locations: Halifax/Dartmouth and the famed Keltic Lodge at Ingonish in Cape Breton. Anne's entire family shared the spotlight on the show which opened with a cameo appearance by

Halifax's unique children's "ukulele band."

Actor Alan Thicke wrote the script for the show and, although the choir members had spoken scripted lines on television before, this show was destined to become an entirely new experience when the group learned that the choir members were also expected to dance with Anne Murray. Hollywood choreographers Jim Bates and his wife, Judy, assured the men that they had "taught football players to dance," so they didn't look upon coal miners as any more of a challenge.

It turned out to be a blast. Dressed in tuxedos and top hats, with pit shovels in hand, The Men danced their way through "Everything Old is New Again" – Anne doing the solo and the men backing her up with vocals and fancy steps. At the conclusion of that scene senior member, Aubrey Martell, representing The Men of the Deeps, presented Anne with a rhinestone-covered mining pick and a pit helmet – also bedecked with rhinestones. Those items were eventually displayed at the very popular Anne Murray Centre in Springhill, and that dance is still floating around in cyberspace somewhere out in "YouTube land."

Fig. 4.5 – Left to right: Jack O'Donnell, Ernie Poirier, Anne Murray, Yogi Muise, Nipper MacLeod, from their dance number during Anne Murray Christmas Special, 1981.

Ann's mother, Marion, was a delight to get to know. She became a good friend and a cherished fan of The Men of the Deeps who never missed a performance whenever the group appeared in Springhill. And it was a special treat for the men, when visiting and performing in Springhill, to meet and get to know, Maurice Ruddick and Caleb Rushton. Maurice, known on the surface as The Singing Miner, kept the spirits of his co-workers alive when the fate of the underground miners seemed so grim during that fateful disaster of 1958. And Caleb, in another section of the mine during that same disaster, did likewise. Caleb's role would eventually be immortalized in one of the verses of Peggy Seeger's famous "Ballad of Springhill." Maurice wrote a song about his experience, which was subsequently collected by Memorial

Fig. 4.6 – Opening refrain of "The Ballad of Springhill." From And Now the Fields are Green, op. cit.

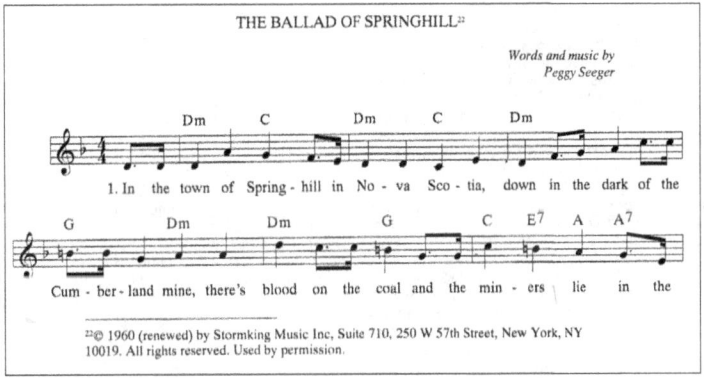

University's Neil Rosenberg and published in the 1992 O'Donnell collection *And Now the Fields are Green*.⁶ Sadly, both Maurice and Caleb are now deceased; Maurice passed away in 1988 and Caleb in 2008.

In 1982, long-time friend and supporter of The Men of the Deeps, Ann Terry MacLellan was made the second honorary member of the all-male choir. Nina Cohen, of course, had merited that honour very early in the history of the choir. Two other prominent females would later have their names added to that roster of honorary members: Springhill's Anne Murray and Cape Breton's Rita MacNeil.⁷

Canada's CANPRO Awards, honouring the best in Canadian television, came to Nova Scotia in 1983, and Cape Breton's Men of the Deeps choir was invited to perform at the Halifax venue. The appearance generated a complimentary editorial in the Canadian edition of *TV Guide*: Describing the group as "one of the world's great choirs," editor Ken Larone was impressed with the stage demeanour of the men, prompting him to conclude: "Their code of life has passed the test of time, and through their music they expose their souls."⁸

The release of The Men of the Deeps third LP recording with Waterloo Music Company came in 1984.⁹ The new album was recorded live the previous summer at the Cape Breton Miners' Museum in Glace Bay during one of the many weekly concerts that feature The Men of the Deeps throughout the summer months. Those summer concerts

Fig. 4.7 – TV Guide, *Maritime Provinces Edition*, n.d.

Fig. 4.8 – The Men of the Deeps' third recording, Waterloo Music.

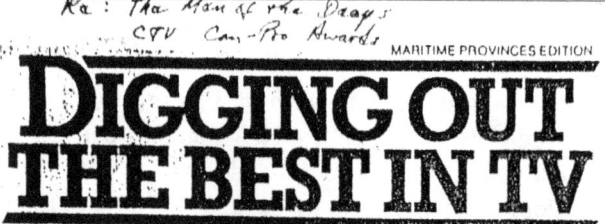

over the years have symbolized a strong bond between the miners choir and the Miners' Museum – both having been born as a result of Canada's Centennial Year, 1967.

It was in 1984 that The Men first performed with beloved Cape Breton songstress, Rita MacNeil. The concert, at Glace Bay's beautiful and historic Savoy Theatre, was a fundraiser for the local hospital. Rita still wore her signature hat in those days, and her band for that concert included Scott Macmillan on lead guitar, with Joella Foulds on guitar and back-up vocals (Joella eventually went on to co-found, with Max MacDonald, Cape Breton's popular *Celtic Colours International Festival*); Ralph Dillon was on keyboards, Allie Bennett on electric base and Halifax musician, John Alphonse, on drums.

Fig. 4.9 – Rita MacNeil, 1995. Publicity photo by Mark Mainguy. Reference number: 95-204-26295. Beaton Institute, Cape Breton University.

Those early concerts with Rita provided a great opportunity for The Men of the Deeps to acquire the knack of spontaneously harmonizing back-up for her lilting melodies. Most successful in that first concert was, of course, the ever-popular "Working Man." In subsequent years, whether the choir was performing with Rita or on its own, popular demand has dictated that neither the chorus nor Rita MacNeil can complete a concert performance without including "Working Man."[10] That 1984 concert was the beginning of a mystical bond between Rita and the men that bloomed for the next three decades.

Fig. 4.10 – Partial score of Rita MacNeil's "Working Man." From And Now the Fields are Green, *op. cit.*

During the 1980s and into the 1990s Cape Breton's singing miners began to attract the attention of some serious promoters. Famed bassoonist, George Zukerman, who ran the concert management Overture Concerts out of Vancouver came up with the slogan "Who are these Men? And what makes their story such an unusual and fascinating one?" And Bob Missen of Robert Missen Artists Management in Toronto entered the scene in the mid 1980s to become one of The Men of the Deeps' most avid supporters and promoters. His company is known today as The Bobolink Agency, and the choir is still very much a favourite on his roster of artists.

Rita MacNeil's tour managers, Brooks Diamond Productions of Halifax, and later Rockland Entertainment's Brian Edwards of Peterborough, Ontario, and Lupins Productions in Cape Breton, headed up by Rita's son, Wade Langham, were all instrumental in advancing the popularity of The Men of the Deeps by making the group an integral part of Rita's many North American tours. Although the choir toured successfully on its own, the "package" of the chorus and Rita MacNeil proved to be a winning combination. Beginning with the highly successful appearances at Vancouver's Expo '86, the ensemble entertained audiences throughout North America right up until her untimely death in 2013.

The New York concert management firm of Gurtman and Murtha Productions later took The Men of the Deeps under its wing resulting in some interesting and very successful concert tours of the southern United States and the Appalachian coal mining areas of Pennsylvania, Virginia and Kentucky. (Those tours will be discussed in Chapter 6.)

In 1986, The Men of the Deeps marked the group's 20th-anniversary year beginning with a concert before an enthusiastic crowd at Halifax's Rebecca Cohn Auditorium.[11] It is interesting to note when reading news coverage of that concert that, in 1986 the ages of the men in the choir ranged from 23 to 80, and that there were eight original members still active in the group. (As the years slowly creep by, the age of the youngest Men of the Deeps choir members has slowly crept up, and in this, the choir's 50th year, the youngest member is in his early fifties!)

Fig. 4.11 – Chronicle Herald, *January, 1986.*

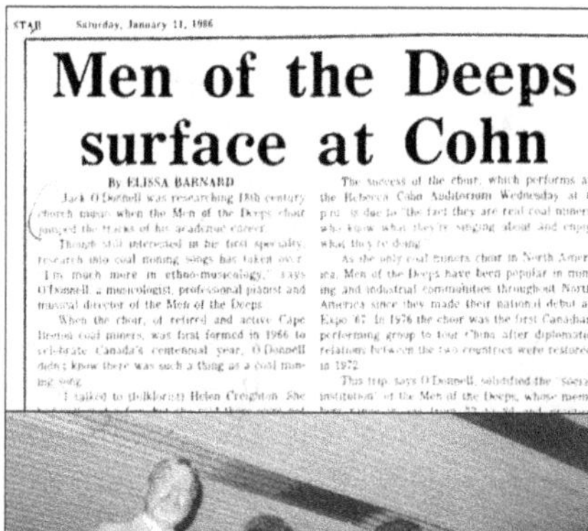

STAR Saturday, January 11, 1986

Men of the Deeps surface at Cohn

By ELISSA BARNARD

Jack O'Donnell was researching 18th century church music when the Men of the Deeps choir jumped the tracks of his academic career.

Though still interested in his first specialty, research into coal mining songs has taken over. "I'm much more in ethno-musicology," says O'Donnell, a musicologist, professional pianist and musical director of the Men of the Deeps.

When the choir, of retired and active Cape Breton coal miners, was first formed in 1966 to celebrate Canada's centennial year, O'Donnell didn't know there was such a thing as a coal mining song.

"I talked to (folklorist) Helen Creighton. She ...

The success of the choir, which performs at the Rebecca Cohn Auditorium Wednesday at 8 p.m., is due to "the fact they are real coal miners who know what they're singing about and enjoy what they're doing."

As the only coal miners choir in North America, Men of the Deeps have been popular in mining and industrial communities throughout North America since they made their national debut at Expo '67. In 1976 the choir was the first Canadian performing group to tour China after diplomatic relations between the two countries were restored in 1972.

This trip, says O'Donnell, solidified the "social institution" of the Men of the Deeps, whose members ...

Fig. 4.12 – Jack and Judy O'Donnell and Anne Terry aboard the Queen Elizabeth II *ocean liner.*

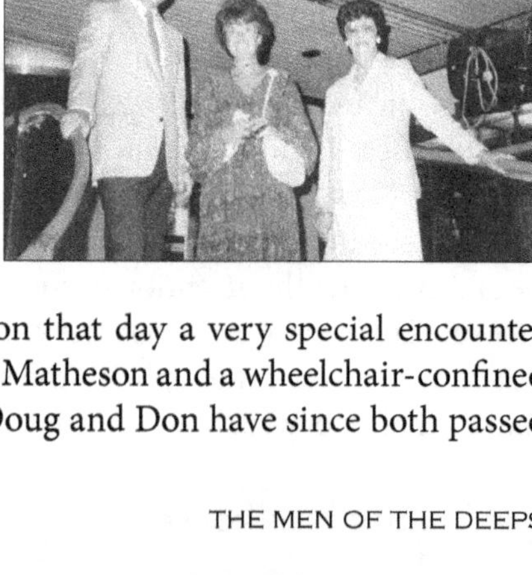

Very few performances could rival a special concert aboard the famous ocean liner *Queen Elizabeth II* when it docked in Sydney Harbour in 1986. One of the successful hallmarks of The Men of the Deeps is the talent of its individual members for chatting with their audiences following a performance, and on that day a very special encounter between tenors Doug Morris and Don Matheson and a wheelchair-confined passenger from England took place. Doug and Don have since both passed away, but that personal encounter between those two choir members (both original members) and Victoria Wignall, a 92-year-old passenger from Brighton, England, reaped an interesting result when, in 1992, Doug received in the mail a cheque for £ 300 (the equivalent in 1992 of $ 637.41). In her accompanying letter, Ms. Wignall said she was "shocked beyond words" when she heard of the May 9 (1992) Westray explosion that trapped 26 men deep in the bowels of the mine. (See more about the Westray Mine disaster in chapter 5.) "I feel so sorry for all the bereaved, and I would like you to give this cheque to any fund set up for the families of the men who died."[12]

Doug Morris obliged Ms. Wignall's wish, travelling to Plymouth, Nova Scotia, and presenting the generous donation to the officials in charge of the fund.[13]

—

Over the years there have been certain individuals who have introduced a special dynamic into the routine performances of The Men of the Deeps. Jim MacLellan is one of those individuals. As previously mentioned, Jim had been away from the choir for several years because of his commitment to DEVCO as manager of No. 26 Colliery in Glace Bay. Jim was deeply moved when he learned that Allister MacGillivray's haunting ballad about the "No. 26 Mine Disaster" was now a part of the choir's repertoire; he is still visibly moved when the choir performs that song. But what gives Jim a wonderful balance is that he also possesses a unique sense of humour. Jim's penchant for telling humourous stories eventually found its way into the performances of The Men of the Deeps, and since his return to the group in 1986 his stories have been an integral part of most concert performances of the choir.

Fig. 4.13 – The Men of the Deeps group photo from Expo '86. Non-chorus performers include Jack O'Donnell, Scott Macmillan, Allie Bennett, Rita MacNeil, John Alphonse and Ralph Dillon. Photo by Siwik Productions.

It was at Expo '86 in Vancouver that the bond between Rita MacNeil and The Men of the Deeps began to blossom. It was at that time also that a particular bond between Rita's guitarist, Scott Macmillan, and the Men also began to take shape. Scott has become a towering figure in the Nova Scotia music community; and as host conductor of Symphony Nova Scotia Maritime Pops for ten years, he introduced The Men of the Deeps and several other Cape Breton artists to the world of symphonic accompaniment. The appearances at Vancouver's Expo '86 proved to

Fig. 4.14 (Right) – On stage at Expo '86, accompanied by the RCMP band.

Fig. 4.15 (Middle) – Cape Breton Post, n.d. Post photo by Ted Rhodes.

Fig. 4.16 (Bottom) – With Rita MacNeil at the Savoy Theatre in Glace Bay, NS.

be very special, in that The Men, in addition to their own series of concerts, were partnered in concerts with Rita MacNeil and the RCMP Concert Band. All of those performances were well-received by multiple audiences and favourably reviewed by the press. Following those Expo appearances The Men of the Deeps and Rita MacNeil went their separate ways to tour other parts of Canada.

The trip en route to Expo '86 had included a stopover at the Sharon Temple near Newmarket, Ontario, where the choir had the pleasure of sharing the stage with popular Celtic singer, Loreena McKennitt. A highlight of that concert was a rendition of one of the oldest songs in the repertoire of The Men of the Deeps, "She Loves Her Miner Lad"[14] which is sung to the tune of the popular Newfoundland folksong, "She's Like the Swallow"; Nipper MacLeod joined Loreena in a duo rendition of the song.

That busy year concluded with a performance before the Canadian Conference of the American Federation of Musicians of the United States and Canada which was meeting in Cape Breton; the choir's performance at the conference was hailed as "most compelling" by the Toronto Symphony Orchestra's Murray Ginsberg.[15]

During the next two years The Men of the Deeps got to know concert halls throughout the Maritime Provinces. The year 1987 saw the men performing at numerous venues from Campbellton, New

Post photo by Ted Rhodes
Men of the Deeps open Centre 200

Brunswick to Alberton, Prince Edward Island, to Baddeck, Nova Scotia. And the group was welcomed at some of the area's unique concert venues including: Sydney's Centre 200 where the men joined a large cast of Nova Scotia performers at the opening of the facility; the beautiful Fredericton Playhouse; Pictou's DeCoste Centre for the Performing Arts; Prince Edward Island's Confederation Centre; and, of course, Glace Bay's historic Savoy Theatre.

With the possible exception of the 1976 tour of China, 1989 was one of the most memorable years to date for The Men of the Deeps. That concert season for the choir began in March with an appearance with Rita MacNeil at the Juno Awards in Toronto. At the Junos, The Men mingled with many of the icons of Canada's musical world: Gordon Lightfoot, k.d. lang, Anne Murray, Jeff Healey, Murray McLauchlan, Blue Rodeo.... And Rita's award-winning song, "Working Man," backed up by The Men of the Deeps, brought the audience to its feet! Even the stage set seemed to have been designed with Rita and her song in mind.

It was an extraordinarily busy year – with the March appearance at the Junos, followed by the Miramichi Folk Festival in New Brunswick in April, a concert appearance with Anne Murray scheduled for July and return performances slated for later in the year at Pictou's DeCoste Centre and Charlottetown's Confederation Centre.

Fig. 4.17 – Newspaper clipping. Source unknown.

Fig. 4.18 (Middle) – Posing with k.d. lang at the Juno Awards in Toronto.

Fig. 4.19 (Below left) – Newspaper clipping reviewing Miramichi festival performance. Source unknown.

4.20 (Below) – Program from Miramichi Folk Song Festival.

The choir had been deeply honoured to receive an invitation from Nicholas Goldschmidt, Artistic Director for the world choral festival to be held in Toronto's Roy Thomson Hall in 1989. Niki had been a friend of The Men of the Deeps since 1975 when he oversaw the sound check for The Men of the Deeps performance at the Canada Day ceremonies on Parliament Hill. The invitation to appear at the 1989 International Choral Festival was indeed something of which the Cape Breton coal miners could be proud.

The opportunity to perform in Toronto's Roy Thomson Hall was an honour in which any amateur choir would take pride, and it turned out to be all that the group could ever expect it to be. Nicholas Goldschmidt had planned the festival as a showcase for many of the world's outstanding choirs, and it was a special honour for The Men of the Deeps to be included as one of Canada's thirty-one choir participants. Chris Dafoe, writing

4.21 (Right) – Cover of festival program. Top right photo is of Nicholas Goldschmidt.

4.22 (Below) – Clippings reviewing festival performance by The Men. The Toronto Star *and* Chronicle Herald.

for Toronto's *Globe and Mail* captioned his very favourable review with the headline "Mining the musical heritage of Cape Breton." (Fig. 4.22)[16] The concert was recorded and in 1991 became the group's first compact disc release.[17]

Upon its return from the International Choral Festival the choir was invited to perform for the opening of the Anne Murray Centre in Anne's beloved Springhill – an invitation which The Men of the Deeps accepted with pride and gratitude.

As the decade drew to a close, Dr. Helen Creighton celebrated her 90th birthday on September 5, 1989. The Men of the Deeps took the opportunity to show appreciation to the folklore icon by sending her a bouquet of twenty-eight roses – representing the twenty-eight singing members of the choir. She had often remarked over the years on a similar gesture from the choir back in 1974 when she was gravely ill, and this gesture on the occasion of her 90th birthday meant a great deal to her. Dr. Creighton's appreciative response was her last communication with the group:

> How kind of you to remember me on my 90th birthday with lovely cards and flowers. The beauty of the flowers, like your treasured friendship, lingers on. And how delightful to have the signatures of all the miners on the card.... I always take great pleasure in hearing them when they perform on radio and television.
>
> Affectionately, Helen Creighton

The Men were deeply saddened to learn of the death of the choir's long-time mentor on December 12, 1982.

Fig. 4.23 – The Globe and Mail, *June 24, 1989, C3,* Globe and Mail *photo by Edward Regan.*

Chapter 5

From the sunken kingdom

To set free a captive prince
From the sunken kingdom of the father coal[1]

In 1991 the Tourism Industry Association of Nova Scotia bestowed its prestigious Ambassador Award on The Men of the Deeps, and an editorial in the Antigonish *Casket*, reflecting on the honour and the twenty-five year history of the singing miners, was one of several media publications to offer sincere congratulations: "You dignify labour. Your lamps illuminate the way to an indigenous culture."[2]

Fig. 5.1 – Diamonds in the Rough: Twenty-five Years with The Men of the Deeps. *Men of the Deeps Music, 1991.*

The award citation stated:

This year, TIANS is proud to acknowledge a group of individuals whose work has become one of Nova Scotia's finest symbols. Their strength lies in the fact that they sing of what they know – the hard lives of the men who have chiselled, blasted and shovelled coal in the mines of Cape Breton since the early 18th Century. While singing of their own lives, and of the people who came before them, they touch a powerful chord in working people everywhere.

It was the 25th-anniversary year and marked by Allister MacGillivray's first documentary publication *Diamonds in the Rough: 25 Years with The Men of the Deeps*. A celebration dinner, as well as Allister's publication, had been prompted and inspired by Sydney business man, the late Harvey Webber, with the assistance of a dedicated and hard-working committee devoted to recognizing the success of Cape Breton's coal miners choir. The choir is deeply indebted to Harvey Webber and the members of that committee[3]; and the choice of Allister MacGillivray to document the first twenty-five years was a wise decision. Allister's experience as a writer, his familiarity with the folk traditions of Cape Breton Island, and his familiarity and admiration for the choir, made him an ideal choice to document the quarter-century achievements of Cape Breton's singing miners.

In the foreword to Allister's publication, Nicholas Goldschmidt (who was in the midst of organizing yet another international choral event in Toronto) sent special greetings and congratulations praising the miners from Cape Breton as "a shining example of what can be achieved by sheer dedication and love for singing."[4]

Group formed 25 years ago

Men of the Deeps help define Cape Breton

By Professor John O'Donnell and Gerry Forbes

THE MEN OF THE DEEPS is a choir of working and retired coal-miners from the island of Cape Breton. Organized in 1966 as part of Cape Breton's contribution to Canada's Centennial Year (1967), their inception was an effort by the people of Cape Breton to preserve in song some of the rich folklore of the island's coal mining communities.

Since 1967 the group has been singing of the work and the lifestyle of the Cape Breton coal miner to audiences throughout most of Canada and parts of the ... ences which include people from many corners of this planet.

In addition to the historical tour to the People's Republic of China, some of the group's interesting concert tours have included two visits to the United States for performances before the United Mine Workers of America at their conventions in Cincinnati, Ohio and Denver, Colordao. In their own country the men have toured the mining communities of Labrador and Northern Manitoba; they have sung in most major centres across Canada and countless smaller towns from coast to coast. The group celebrated its 20th anniversary year with a successful 2½ week en- ...

... loo, Ontario. Present plans for the release of a Men of the Deeps Live Concert recording to mark the group's 25th anniversary year in 1991.

The Men of the Deeps are no strangers to the media. They have appeared in two films produced by the National Film Board of Canada. They have been heard frequently on CBC radio in Canada and their list of television performances includes Canada's popular Front Page Challenge, Canadian Express and Take Thirty. In 1982 they were special guests on the Anne Murry Christmas Special seen throughout North America on the CBS and CTV television networks. In 1986 the CTV network did a special documentary honor- ...

... must have worked in the mines ... ages of the men range from ... about one-third of which have been ... the group since it was organized in ... A special sense of authenticity is g... to the group by the presence of se... retired coal miners who recall ... the days when coal miners were lo... upon as "second class" citizens, fo... to eke out a living mining coal in haz... ous conditions while their lives were ... most entirely dependent upon the c... pany.

Today The Men of the Deeps is m... than a singing group — it's a social in... tution, too. There is a camarade... amongst the members of the group t... carries over to their audiences ...

'When you go to Men of Deeps you'd better take a hanky'

To many a working and former miner, the words to Rita MacNeil's Working ...

80s ... is one of the few instances where union and management are comfortable on the same stage together.

Rita MacNeil ... and several other television shows.

"If the people in the front row feel good, then that makes you feel good."

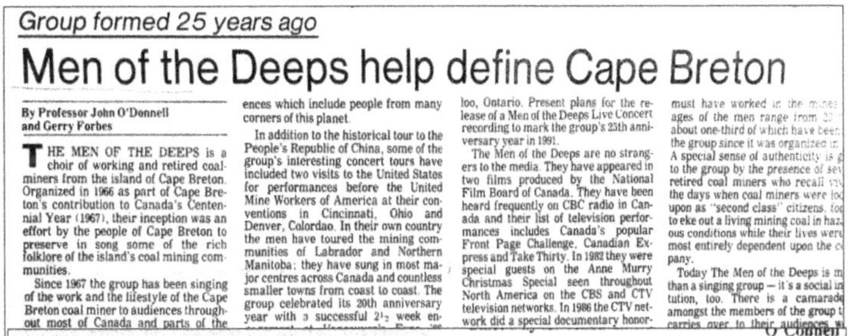

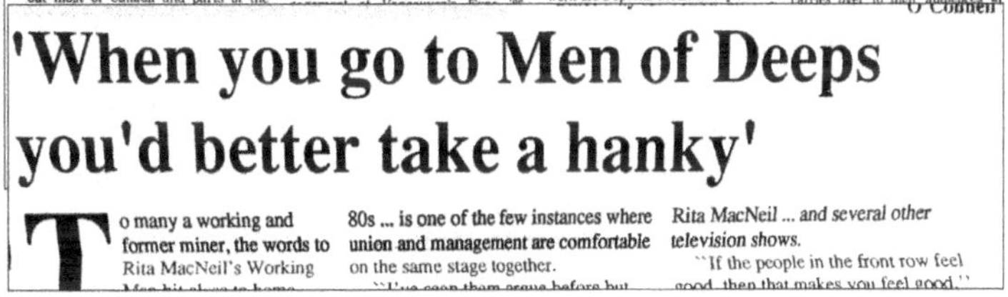

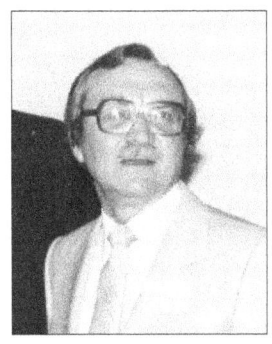

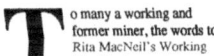

Fig. 5.2 (Top) – Cape Breton businessman and philanthropist, Harvey Webber (d. 2003), 1982. Photographer unknown. (Detail) reference number: 98-746-29533. Beaton Institute, Cape Breton University.

Fig. 5.3 (Middle) – Source unknown.

Fig. 5.4 (Lower) – Source unknown.

Although the 1990s were destined to become the busiest to date for the choir, great sadness came early in the decade when, on May 9, 1992, twenty-six miners lost their lives in an explosion at the Westray Mine in Plymouth, Nova Scotia – the nearby mining towns of New Glasgow, Stellarton, Westville and Trenton were deeply affected.

The choir had been booked for a concert that very evening in Antigonish – some 50 km from the site of the ill-fated mine. Performing for that concert was not easy for the group. Several of the choir members had friends and family involved in the rescue operations. Jim MacLellan, Jr., son of founding member Jim MacLellan, was one of fifty-seven Cape Breton draegermen[5] and miners involved in the dangerous and ultimately futile rescue attempt. They were later honoured at an Award for Bravery celebration in Stellarton. In an effort to reach out, the choir donated its fee for that performance to whatever relief fund might be set up for the survivors of the tragedy.

Al Provoe, another of the founding members of The Men of the Deeps and known for his talent with words, wrote a poem in the days following that performance; he dedicated it to the surviving family members and the men who lost their lives:

Aftermath
There are tears today around Westray;
They have a hurt, the pain shall stay.
The dust of coal and cruel methane
Destroyed a driving bid for gain.

With drill and loader close at hand
He'd bore and scrape and watch and plan.
He feared the roof stone, hanging tough,
That sometimes crashed mid'st clouds of dust.

No want for haste now, sweat or speed,
To bolt a room for safety need,
To aid the quest of man for wealth,
Who operate with ken and stealth.

And now these colliery men from home
Shall never see their family grown.
Shall nevermore hear tiny feet
That ran to greet them from the street.

Devastated, anxious, sad –
We rue the chance they never had.
We damn the need to place a blame,
When all you have is down the drain.

But morning sun will rise again,
As sure the roosters crow,
And man will toil beneath the
    soil,
Where 'er the coal seams grow.

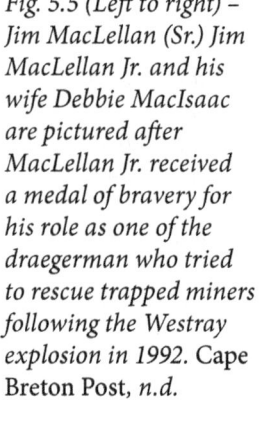

Fig. 5.5 (Left to right) – Jim MacLellan (Sr.) Jim MacLellan Jr. and his wife Debbie MacIsaac are pictured after MacLellan Jr. received a medal of bravery for his role as one of the draegerman who tried to rescue trapped miners following the Westray explosion in 1992. Cape Breton Post, n.d.

The days and weeks following the Westray explosion were difficult times for Nova Scotia's mining communities – and for Nova Scotians in general. The controversy, accusations, the court proceedings and their aftermath, simply contributed to prolonging the pain and reality of the situation. Cape Breton's Men of the Deeps played a prominent part in the remembrances and memorial services in the days following the tragedy, and to this day the men who lost their lives and the surviving families are regularly remembered wherever and whenever the group performs.

One of the most poignant songs to emerge in the days and weeks following the disaster was composed by Ron MacDonald, of New Glasgow, and originally performed by his own Pictou County group, Déjà vu. "Their Lights Will Shine" is a moving tribute to the memory of the twenty-six unsuspecting coal miners who lost their lives in a disaster that never should have happened.[6] The song is still a favourite when performed in concert, preceded by Al Provoe's poem, "Aftermath."

It was later in 1992 that the first major collection of coal mining songs in Canada was published: *And Now the Fields are Green: A Collection of Coal Mining Songs in Canada*.[7] The title of the collection is taken from the final verse of another of Al Provoe's sensitive poems, "Who Are They?"

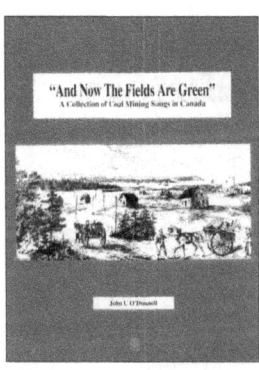

Fig. 5.6 – And Now the Fields are Green, *op. cit.*

> Who are they who fought to break the company chain
> And never shied when days were lean
> To change this way of life?
> And now the fields are green.

Making note of the recent tragic explosion at the Westray Mine, the book comments on the dramatic increase in the awareness of the dangers and hardships associated with the coal mining industry precipitated by the publicity surrounding the Westray tragedy – making note also that at the same time, the wide publicity accorded this event has demonstrated to the world the camaraderie, compassion and love which characterize the special breed of human beings who live in Canada's coal mining communities.

Prominent persons in the field of folklore who offered endorsements of the publication included Edith Fowke (editor of the *Canadian Folk Music Journal*), Archie Green (retired professor of folklore, University of Texas) and Joe Glazer (popular folksinger and chairman of the Labor Heritage Foundation in Washington, DC).

Anne Murray returned to Nova Scotia in 1992 for another television special. Filmed on the spectacular Cabot Trail in Cape Breton, the show featured guests Rita MacNeil, The Rankin Family, The Gospel Heirs and The Men of the Deeps, all of whom joined Anne in a moving finale featuring Leon Dubinsky's popular Cape Breton anthem, "Rise Again" – filmed by swirling heli-

Fig. 5.7 – *With the famous Cabot Trail in the background, The Men pose with Rita MacNeil during the taping of an Anne Murray TV special.*

Fig. 5.8 – Jack O'Donnell addresses the audience at a Red Cross Light Up the Darkness concert, with the provincial children's choir and The Men of the Deeps in the background.

copters capturing the beauty of the surrounding countryside.

—

Members of The Men of the Deeps, all being fathers and family men, have always related to young people. So, it was a special privilege, in 1994, when the group was asked by Louise Simon, a talented Halifax musician and president of the Halifax Chapter of the Canadian Red Cross, to do a fundraising tour for the Red Cross featuring The Men of the Deeps and schoolchildren's choir's from around the province. The "Light Up the Darkness" tour was so successful that the tour was expanded and repeated in 1996 and again in 1998. The men still take delight when they are occasionally greeted following a concert by a young adult who recalls singing with The Men of the Deeps when they were in grade school.

Throughout the 1980s and 1990s the group continued to take advantage of its popularity in Western Canada, and also to explore much of the area in and around Ontario's Nickel Belt region. Probably the most exhausting of all the trips was the journey to the town of Manitouwadge in 1995. Located in Ontario's Thunder Bay district, the commitment to visit and perform in the town subjected the group to a thirteen-hour (overnight) drive by bus from Toronto's Pearson International Airport – a trip rivalled only by another lengthy journey that had taken place several years earlier: the trip to the town of Swan Lake in northern Manitoba subjected the men to several hours on a dirt road. It is a credit to each and every member of the group that their love of singing and meeting fellow Canadians overrides any exhaustion they might feel.

In the mid 1990s The Men of the Deeps were asked by Robert Missen Artists Management and Algoma University in Sault Ste. Marie, Ontario, to take part in a celebration honouring Nicholas Goldschmidt's long career as a supporter and promoter of the arts in Canada. It was, of course, an honour to have been asked. The appearance of The Men was to be a surprise for Niki, so members of the choir were caught off guard when they boarded the small plane out of Toronto to find Niki and his wife, Shelagh, sitting at the front of the plane. Niki did not suspect that the men might be involved in his celebration – and members of the choir, much to their credit, kept the secret.

There are stories, of course, which relate to every venture involving concert tours by The Men of the Deeps; one, in particular, involving ground transportation, is worth recalling. Travelling long distances by plane and having to pile on to a bus to get to an appointed destination is tiring at the best of times, but the circumstance which presented itself en route to Ontario's popular Elora Festival in Guelph tops the chart.

Manoeuvering one's way through the then recently improved Pearson International Airport in Toronto can be extremely tiring for a group of men (many of them well past the age of sixty-five) who are also responsible for transporting gear worn on stage and musical equipment along with their own mining outfits. So members of the group were, of course, expecting a rather sizeable up-class vehicle to meet them at the airport. What pulled up to the departure dock this time was a visibly worn and over-used school bus. There appeared to be no choice but to accept the situation at hand and see what change could be made after reaching the destination. The scene was one right out of *The Beverly Hillbillies*! By the time everything was loaded, there was very little room for thirty-two "sizeable" men. Paul White, our guitarist at the time, summed the situation up when he commented: "All we need now is a few chickens flapping around, and maybe a goat or two on the roof!" Apparently, there had been a communications misunderstanding that originated with the festival organizers. A call to Bob Missen saw to it that things were fixed up quickly, and the remainder of the tour went without a hitch.

The Men of the Deeps start a summer tour of Ontario by singing at the Elora Festival next week

Mining and singing blend in harmony

BY VALERIE HILL
THE GUELPH MERCURY

Overalls, a hard hat, work boots and day old stubble is not the usual garb of musical

Francis Xavier University in Antigonish, Nova Scotia.

O'Donnell has been travelling the weekly 300 mile round trip to Glace Bay where he works with the group for most of its 28-year

It is this entangling of music with genuine pain, and sometimes happiness, that always draws a response from the audience. The tears flow quietly, even from those who have never known the

as Rita MacNeil and Anne Murray. They have toured the People's Republic of China the US and in January of this year began a Canadian tour, Light the Darkness which hopes to promote awareness of the

Fig. 5.9 (Above) – The Guelph Mercury, *n.d.*

Fig. 5.10 (Below) – Program from Yorkton Arts Council concert.

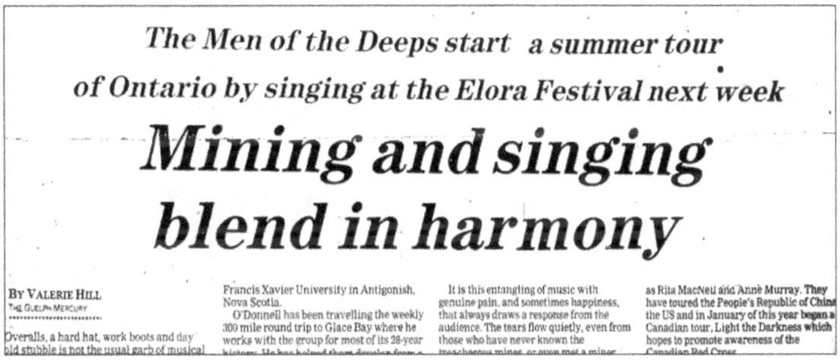

The Toronto/Elora fiasco was a far cry from the receptions we had received in The People's Republic of China back in 1976. On that tour, upon arriving at our first concert destination, the group was met with, not only a modern bus, but also a special limousine (with curtains on each side to side window) assigned to the musical director. It was, of course, a source of embarrassment for the director who, rather than insult the hosts by declining, requested that at least two other members of the group should ride in the limo as well. (The limousine was dispensed with for the remainder of the tour, and all comfortably travelled together by bus or train.)

The latter part of the 1990s saw The Men of the Deeps join Rita MacNeil on her successful television series *Rita and Friends.* Popular singer Roger Whitaker invited the choir to sing backup on his album *Awakening*, and the group had the honour of appearing with the Bach-Elgar Choir, John Allan Cameron and the family of recently deceased folk icon, Stan Rogers, in

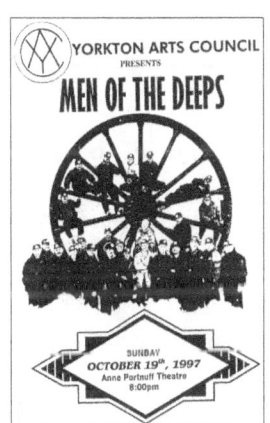

Fig. 5.11 – Hamilton Spectator, *Nov. 1996.*

Fig. 5.12 – The Toronto Star, *April 21, 1999.* Toronto Star *photo by Peter Power.*

"A Celtic Celebration" at Ontario's Hamilton Place. And, somehow, The Men of the Deeps found time to tour Western Canada in 1997[8] and Newfoundland in 1998.[9]

Before the decade came to an end, the group enjoyed a special thrill when The Men were invited to sing the national anthems at a Toronto Blue Jays game in what was then known as the Skydome. Wherever The Men of the Deeps perform there are always Cape Bretoners in the audience; the Skydome was no exception. As the group paraded on to the field, a fan was heard to yell: "Hey, Big Jim!" It was, of course, a fan from Glace Bay. The whole experience was thrilling for the group, but they had to take rain checks on the free tickets offered for the gig. That same evening the choir recorded a performance before a live audience at CBC's Glenn Gould Studio – located just across the street from the Skydome. (The men were able to use those complimentary baseball tickets on the following evening.)

The Men of the Deeps released two CDs on the Atlantica label during the 1990s: *Buried Treasures*, was a compilation of many of the songs originally released on the Waterloo LP recordings. Clyde Gilmour (CBC Sunday afternoons *Gilmour's Albums*) was particularly fond of this compilation; he would often phone seeking information about the songs. Readers who might remember *Gilmour's Albums* will recall his familiar radio introduction: "Hello! My name is Clyde Gilmour, and this is *Gilmour's Albums*." In a similar fashion, particularly if he had to leave a message, his phone calls always began with the familiar salutation: "Hello! My name is Clyde Gilmour!"

Coal Fire in Winter was a very special CD release; because of the unique acoustics, much of it was recorded in the chapel at Fortress Louisbourg by Island Recording and Productions of Frenchvale, Cape Breton. This CD was produced by Allister MacGillivray and featured cover artwork, by Carol Kennedy depicting the inside of a stone dwelling (typical of those at Fortress Louisbourg) with a warming fire in an open fireplace.

Carol Kennedy's artwork was designed to complement industrial folk poet Thomas McGrath's poem, "Coal Fire in Winter," which also is depicted as part of the cover artwork.

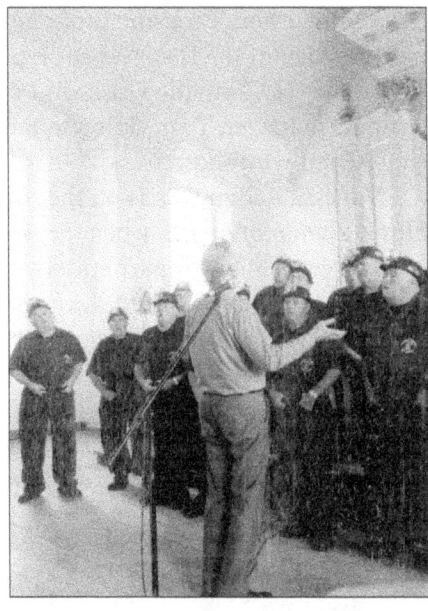

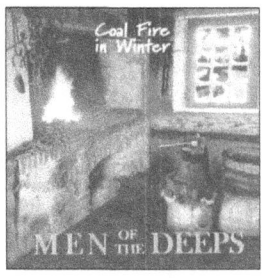

Fig. 5.13 (Left) – The Men recording in the chapel at Fortress of Louisbourg National Historic Site.

Fig. 5.14 (Above) – Coal Fire in Winter, *Atlantica.*

Fig. 5.15 (Below) – Cape Breton Post, *Sept. 4, 1996.*

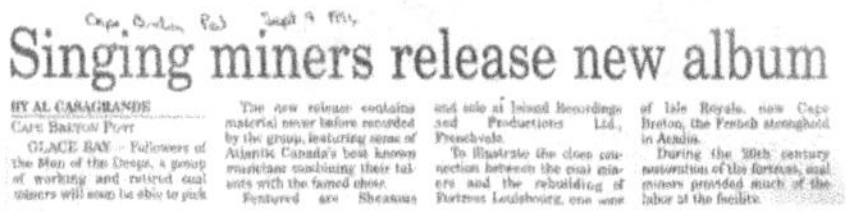

Singing miners release new album

BY AL CASAGRANDE
Cape Breton Post

GLACE BAY – Followers of the Men of the Deeps, a group of working and retired coal miners will soon be able to pick

The new release contains material never before recorded by the group, featuring some of Atlantic Canada's best known musicians combining their talents with the famed choir.

Featured are [illegible] and sale at Island Recordings and Productions Ltd., Frenchvale.

To illustrate the close connection between the coal miners and the rebuilding of Fortress Louisbourg, one [illegible] of Isle Royale, now Cape Breton, the French stronghold in Acadia.

During the 20th century restoration of the fortress, coal miners provided much of the labor at the facility.

Coal Fire in Winter

Something old and tyrannical burning there
(Not like wood fire which is only
The end of a summer or a life)
But something of darkness: heat
From the time before there was fire.
And I have come here
To set free a captive prince
From the sunken kingdom of the father coal.

A warming company of the cold – blooded –
These carbon serpents of bituminous gardens
These inflammable tunnels of dead song
From the black pit

This sparkling end
Of the great beasts, these blazing
Stone flowers diamond fire incandescent fruit.
And out of all that death, now
At midnight, my love and I are riding
Down the old high roads of inexhaustible light.[10]

—

It was June 1999: A routine summer with a routine summer concert schedule. The Men of the Deeps were preparing for an outdoor July performance to be held on Granville Green in Port Hawkesbury. It was not routine for business manager, Yogi Muise, to receive a phone call from a British Academy Award winning actress.

Vanessa Redgrave was on the south shore of Nova Scotia, working on a film, *A Rumor of Angels,* when she was introduced to a recording of The Men of the Deeps. She was particularly intrigued with the idea that these were ordinary, working people.[11] Learning from her phone call with business manager Yogi Muise that the group was scheduled for a July appearance in Port Hawkesbury, she immediately made plans to attend in person.

Renowned for her efforts to improve the conditions of the young and the poor in troubled lands, in 1995 she had been appointed UNICEF Special Representative for the Performing Arts.[12] In this capacity, she was in the process of organizing a special festival to be held in Pristina, Kosovo – a festival aimed at welcoming home the many Albanian refugees who had been driven from the former Yugoslav province by then President Milosevic's troops as part of the government's ethnic cleansing.

She showed up at the concert that July afternoon and was apparently moved by the performance to the point that she announced to the audience, following the concert, that she would like The Men of the Deeps to join her and a host of talented performers from around the world at "The Return," an international festival of music and theatre to be held in Pristina, Kosovo, in September 1999.

With overwhelming support from Hon. Lloyd Axeworthy, Canada's Minister of External Affairs at the time, and with the backing of a host of patrons (which included Mikhail Baryshnikov, Meryl Streep, Elton John, Sting and U2's Bono), The Men of the Deeps departed for Kosovo on September 7, 1999. And since the situation in Kosovo was still somewhat volatile (troops and police from many countries, including Canada, were still patrolling the streets and countryside), Vanessa and the entertainers were to stay in Skopje, Macedonia, from

Fig. 5.16 (Above) – The Men pose with Vanessa Redgrave at Port Hawkesbury' Granville Green.

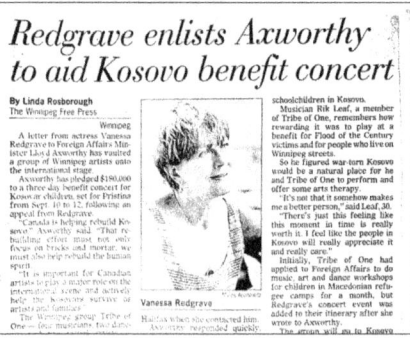

Fig. 5.17 – Winnipeg Free Press, *n.d.*

where they would commute daily to Prestina, Kosovo. This, indeed, was unlike any tour the choir had ever experienced.

The group's flight plan took them via London and Zurich to Skopje, Macedonia. They had been prepped on the unsettled conditions in Kosovo, so the excitement of the moment was somewhat tempered by the uncertainty that might await them during the next few days. While flying over France, a request

Fig. 5.18, 5.19 – Maps.

Fig. 5.20 (Right) – Armoured vehicle near Kosovo.

Fig. 5.21 (Middle) – The Men disembark in Skopje.

Fig. 5.22 (Bottom) – Jack O'Donnell with Bruce Cockburn.

from the Swiss Air flight attendants to sing for the passengers was welcomed, and one of the impressionable moments of the trip was singing "Down Deep in a Coal Mine" while flying over the Eiffel Tower on the descent into Zurich where the men were to change planes for the final leg of the flight to Skopje.

Ms. Redgrave was there to meet The Men when they arrived at the Grand Hotel in Skopje – as was Canadian singer Bruce Cockburn who had been booked into the same hotel. The host of performers who would be taking part in the festival was impressive.

Entertainers and members of the entertainment groups accompanying Vanessa to a press conference were also given a tour of Pristina's National Theatre where some of the concerts were to take place. All were visibly moved when encountering an array of graffiti on the outside wall of the theatre (see fig. 5.23). The graffiti was actually an expression of thanks from the people of Kosovo to the many world leaders who had been instrumental

FROM THE SUNKEN KINGDOM

Fig. 5.23 – Post-war graffiti on Pristina's National Theatre.

in bringing the war to an end. What really touched all was the humble spelling of the names of the world leaders. "THANK YOU!", the graffiti read: "NATO, TONI BLER, KLINTON, SHRODER, ROBIN KUK, SHIRAK, OLBRIGHT"[13] and others.

It was somewhat of a disappointment when, on the following day, the performers arrived at the theatre to find the graffiti freshly painted over; no sign of the thank you message remained.

Day one of the festival, September 10, was held in Skopje's Universal Hall and featured American composer Philip Glass and African ethnic composer Foday Musa Suso, originally from The Gambia. On day two, September 11, the festival moved to Pristina's National Theatre with a piano recital by holocaust survivor Katharina Wolpe, and performances by Japanese violinist Akiko Ono, America's Martha Graham Dance Company and a play by noted Albanian actor Enver Petrovci.

A Saturday evening open-air jazz extravaganza would be introduced by Italian movie star Franco Nero and would include Italian actress, Mara Venier, the Lino Patruno Jazz Show and Italian singer-songwriter, Andrea Mingardi, who would be joined by Albanian, Ilir Bajri, and his Kosovar jazz band, Quasi Fusion.

The finale at Pristina's Great Hall opened with a chorus of 200 Kosovar children, with South African musician Lebo M, singing his arrangement of Elton John's "The Lion King."[14] Vanessa Redgrave and her mother, Lady Rachel Kempson, were also featured with selected recitations, and performances by renowned French singer Patricia Kaas, British star Lulu and the popular band Big Country, Canadian performers Bruce Cockburn, Winnipeg's Tribe of One and Cape Breton's coal miners choir.

Vanessa Redgrave's desire to include The Men in this array of international performers was driven by the realization that it was the coal miners in Kosovo who were instrumental in the first demonstrations against President Milosovic's policies, prompting him to send in the military forces. Because of this unique connection, she explained, Canada's The Men of the Deeps coal miners chorus played a pivotal role in the festival.

Perhaps one of the most memorable performances in the entire fifty-year history of The Men of the Deeps happened at that final concert extravaganza in Pristina. "When The Men made their entrance[15] with their helmet lamps blazing, what greeted them was a spontaneous ovation from the Kosovars who understood the significance of the Cape Breton miners' appearance."[16]

> It was an extremely moving concert. When The Men of the Deeps performed 'Rise Again' the young people in the audience were waving their arms and you could see tears running down the eyes of some of them. People were waving their lighters in rhythm to the music. It was a tremendous experience.[17]

As mentioned above, some of the entertainers, including members from The Men of the Deeps, had accompanied Ms. Redgrave to a major press conference at Pristina's Grand Hotel early on the first day of the festival. The press conference, with a host of reporters representing press agencies from around the world, had been organized by the United Nations Children's Fund (UNICEF) and the United Nations High Commissioner for Refugees (UNHCR); it gave Redgrave an opportunity to stress that the true meaning of the "Return Festival" was to celebrate the restoration of Kosovo's cultural and artistic life: "We are not only celebrating the return of the province's artists and performers," she told them, "but we are also promoting the return of tolerance and respect among the different communities. Art and music cannot exist in a climate of hatred, and everyone across Kosovo must now work together to rebuild both their communities and their trust for each other."[18]

Vanessa had been very moved by the emotion of the poem "Coal Fire in Winter." She had been given the CD as a gift when she met The Men of the Deeps in July and carried the CD with her to Kosovo. Members of the choir who were present at the press conference were pleasantly surprised and very pleased when she chose to conclude her remarks by reciting the poem for the world media. In her words, the Thomas McGrath poem expressed in a particularly poignant way the reason she had brought artists and entertainers from around the world to Kosovo. She concluded by reciting the poem for the world media.

As is always the case, The Men of the Deeps made many friends in Kosovo – especially among young people. The holding area for the group was a large gymnasium attached to the concert venue. It was even large enough for a medium-sized tent which served as a dressing room area for Vanessa and her mother, Lady Rachel. And there was still room for some young Kosovar children to toss a basketball around.

Throughout its history, The Men of the Deeps have always bonded closely with the children – whether it be at a concert in the Miners' Museum in Glace Bay where the young people in the audience often gather as a group on the floor in front of the choir, or in a concert such as those that comprised the "Light the Darkness" series where numerous school choirs joined in on such standards as "Working Man," "Rise Again" or "Song for the Mira."

In China, there were countless encounters with young people – especially when the group visited schools, or when the young staff members in the various hotels would join the men in song following a concert performance. Many of those encounters are documented in Silver Donald Cameron's series of *Weekend Magazine* articles.

Kosovo was no different. There was much down-time during the afternoon rehearsals. Patiently waiting in the gymnasium holding area, it seemed natural for some members of The Men to toss a basketball or two with the young people who were also waiting to be called to the stage for a rehearsal session. There was a very poignant scene when second tenor, Billy MacPherson, taught a group of the children to sing a few bars of "Dust in the Air," a popular arrangement in the choir's repertoire. It was a delightful

Fig. 5.24 – Choir member Jude Kelly with children outside the rehearsal hall.

and moving experience to be entertained by the children, with lighted mining helmets (borrowed from The Men) on their heads, singing the familiar song for those gathered around at the time. Such is the charisma of The Men of the Deeps!

The many adventures of the 1990s came to a fitting end in October when the choir, along with Rita MacNeil, embarked on its first tour south of the border. That tour – which took the choir to Scranton, Pennsylvania, Berea, Kentucky, Port Huron, Michigan, and Buffalo, New York – was the precursor of what was to become the "Mining the Soul" series of concert tours featuring Rita MacNeil and The Men of the Deeps. It also marked the beginning of a long and productive relationship between The Men and the talented musicians who provided the instrumental backup for Rita MacNeil: Jeff Arsenault on drums, Bruce Dixon on bass, Chris Corrigan on guitar and the multi-talented Kim Dunn on keyboards. The "Mining the Soul" concert tours were destined to traverse the Canadian landscape almost annually throughout the last twelve years of Rita MacNeil's career.

Fig. 5.25 – Hamilton Spectator, *Nov. 28, 2000.* Hamilton Spectator photo by Barry Gray.

Chapter 6

Mining the musical heritage of Cape Breton

The year was 2000; the reality of the end of the Cape Breton Development Corporation and the centuries-old coal mining industry had finally set in. Silver Donald Cameron, reflecting on his days with The Men of the Deeps in China, paid homage to an industry that gave Cape Breton its soul: "What is lost in the closing of the Cape Breton mines is not merely an outmoded industry," he wrote, "but a heroic and mythic story, with its own social order, its own giants, its own family sorrows, its own culture. These are splendid men, and this is the end of their story."[1]

The end of their mining story, yes – but the rich culture of Cape Breton's coal mining communities has not been forgotten. Nina Cohen and Dr. Helen Creighton knew that this day would eventually come; that is why they wanted a choir of coal miners – so that the "heartbeat" could go on in songs and stories.

The Men of the Deeps felt the pain when in September 1999, Phalen colliery closed for good, with 400 employees laid off and the only on-line-traffic source for the DEVCO coal railway severed. The Prince

Fig. 6.1 – Chronicle Herald, *n.d.*

colliery closed for good on November 23, 2001, after the federal government failed to entice any private sector investors to purchase the mine. And on December 18, 2001, DEVCO sold all of its surface assets.

As we entered the new millennium, Cape Bretoners showed their appreciation for the contributions of The Men of the Deeps and offered encouragement for the choir to keep that heartbeat going. On May 13, 2000, Cape Breton University bestowed the degree Doctor of Letters (*honoris causa*) on the entire group. (That same degree had been conferred upon the director in 1993.) And on May 14 the name of The Men of the Deeps was added to the "Walk of Stars" at Glace Bay's Savoy Theatre prompting Prime Minister Jean Chretien, in his congratulatory message, to recognize the "unique view into Cape Breton's mining heritage" provided by The Men performances around the world: "I commend you for your commitment to ensuring that this heritage is not only preserved but celebrated."[2]

Fig. 6.2 – The Men of the Deeps Star, Savoy Theatre, Glace Bay, NS.

Fig. 6.3 – Cape Breton University honorary degree recipients. CBU photo by Warren Gordon.

Fig. 6.4 – The Continuing Saga, *by Allister MacGillvray. Men of the Deeps Music, 2000.*

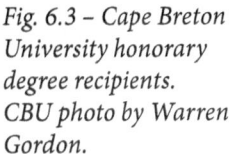

Because of the mine closures, Nipper MacLeod, a long-time member of the choir, had to leave the mines just shy of a pension. Following the honorary degree ceremony at Cape Breton University, when asked if he might be applying for a job at the new call centre, in typical Men of the Deeps humour, he replied: "I won't need to. I'm going to be a doctor!"

The Men of the Deeps, The Continuing Saga, Allister MacGillivray's publication documenting the 35-year history of The Men of the Deeps was published in the year 2000 as a follow-up to his publication ten years earlier, *Diamonds in the Rough*. Both books are unique in their approach, documenting not only the history of the choir, but also a special insight into the personalities of the men who make up its membership.

Award ceremonies behind them, The Men of the Deeps proceeded with performances around the local area, including the yearly summer concerts at the Miners' Museum, before embarking on another extensive

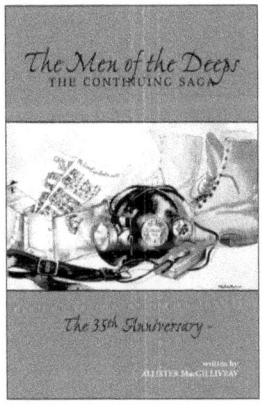

Fig. 6.5 – *Chronicle Herald*, n.d.

> **Men of Deeps mark 35 years**
> *Recent Kosovo trip among miners' most memorable performances*
>
> By Andrea Nemetz
> Entertainment Reporter
>
> Dominion's Bill MacPherson was a coal miner as was his father and grandfather before him.
> And the father of three, who retired six months ago after 27 [...] Cape Breton in recognition of their contribution to Cape Breton culture.
> On Saturday the Men of the Deeps will celebrate their 35th anniversary with a gala dinner at the Bayplex in Glace Bay. Native son Daniel Petrie, an award-win[...] initiated by Albanian coal miners who refused to leave the mines when the Serbs expelled them, so there was a connection," said Fred Gillis, a 10-year choir member who is president of Men of the Deeps.
> "We were there for a week, staying in Macedonia and commuting in and out by bus. Bruce Cockburn was there and many other artists (composer Philip Glass, British country rock band Big Country and the Martha [...] that claimed the lives of [...] Gillis, a lead tenor w[...] the No. 26 colliery as w[...] Lingan, Prince and Phel[...] from 1982 to 1995 when [...] the provincial Depart[...] Community Services.
> "Being a coal miner always aware of the gr[...] admired what they did, confidence level was su[...] didn't think I was good e[...] be with them," said the D[...] native who is married

tour of Ontario – beginning with a performance in Montreal. It was on this tour that the group was invited by Bob Missen to perform for a special concert celebrating the 60th birthday of Sylvia Tyson – followed by a party for the Canadian folk icon at Missen's home.

On November 4, 2000, the choir was honoured by the community yet again at a gala dinner inspired, once again, by Sydney business man, Harvey Webber, with the help of a diligent committee.[3] Guest speaker, Hollywood film director Daniel Petrie was, at the last minute, unable to attend because of a serious illness, and Senator Al Graham, long-time friend and supporter of The Men of the Deeps willingly stepped in.[4] The Men will be forever grateful to the late Senator Al Graham for his lifetime of support for the group and for all of Nova Scotia.

On the day following that gala celebration the group left with Rita MacNeil on a cross-country "Mining the Soul" tour that took them from Kingston, Ontario, to Vancouver, British Columbia, arriving home on December 14 (after a nineteen-city concert tour) just in time to enjoy the Christmas season with their families. The tours were destined to bring the message of Cape Breton's coal mining heritage to cities throughout this vast country from Newfoundland to Ontario and the Prairie Provinces and on to British Columbia, often billed as "A Mining the Soul Christmas."

Early in 2001 Canadian film producer and cinematographer, John Walker, expressed an interest in producing a documentary centred around the closing of the mines in Cape Breton. Walker travelled with the choir on several concert tours throughout 2001 and 2002. The end result was a very moving film, *The Men of the Deeps,* featuring the chorus and several of their co-workers – all of whom were deeply affected by the decision to close the mines for good and the realization that the Cape Breton Development Corporation had effectively ceased all operations.

The film, directed by John Walker and produced by the National Film Board of Canada in association with Picture Plant and John Walker Productions, had its

Fig. 6.6 (Below) – *Cape Breton Post*, Dec. 18, 2003. Photo courtesy John Walker Productions.

> **Last days of coal**
> Shot during the dying days of Devco, Men of the Deeps documentary lovingly tells miners' story

Fig. 6.7 (Left) – Cape Breton Post, *June 6, 2002.*

Fig. 6.8 (Below left) – Chronicle Herald, Dec. 12, 2003. Photo courtesy NFB.

Fig. 6.9 (Below middle) - Photo courtesy John Walker Productions.

Fig. 6.10 (Below right) – Director John Walker (left) with chorus member Ike Lambert. Photo courtesy John Walker Productions.

premier showing in Toronto and went on to win three Gemini awards: Best Performing Arts, Best Documentary Photography and Best Sound. The film also merited a Best Director nomination and garnered three million viewers in Canada alone in the year that it was released. It has been aired several times on various television networks since 2003.

The Men of the Deeps affiliation with Vanessa Redgrave did not end in Kosovo. In the spring of 2001 she came to Nova Scotia again – this time to accept an honorary degree from St. Francis Xavier University.[5] Before leaving Kosovo, The Men of the Deeps had presented her with a unique Cape Breton souvenir: A "Cape Breton Passport." Little did the group understand at the time the deep meaning this would have for her when it came to her passion concerning world suppression and poverty.

In her convocation address (which was given spontaneously, without notes) she began by showing the graduates and their families and friends in the audience her newly acquired "Cape Breton Passport." Although she was obviously aware that the document was a souvenir for the benefit of visiting tourists, she nevertheless had decided to use it as a prop for the message she wanted to deliver. "Many people in this world do not own, nor can they get, a passport," she began as she launched into a revealing dissertation on the plight of the world's downtrodden. Once again, to illustrate her point to the graduates (like in her dissertation to the international press in Pristina), she chose to conclude her address by reciting the poem "Coal Fire in Winter."[6] Her point was well made and well received. It was revealed later that her entire convocation address had been broadcast live on National Public Radio in the United States. Despite her extremely busy schedule in May of 2001, she was able to spend two full days in Antigonish meeting intimately with drama and literature students before delivering a very challenging and provocative convocation address.

The summer of 2001 brought a cherished opportunity to The Men of the Deeps when the group was asked to perform for "Suas e!," a summer festival for youth choirs held in Sydney, and sponsored by the Nova Scotia Choral Federation. As was always the case, the rapport established between The Men and the young people was special, prompting one 15-year old youth to comment: "WOW! Through their (The Men of the Deeps) music I saw a whole new culture, even in my own country. How different it is out east even from southwestern Ontario."[7]

Fig. 6.11 – Program from 2002 performance with Symphony Nova Scotia.

And in that same year, Halifax musician and guest conductor of Symphony Nova Scotia, Scott Macmillan, collaborated with the chorus on a project that would culminate in a gala concert in March 2002 featuring the symphony, the choir and Cape Breton fiddling icon, Buddy MacMaster. It took months of preparation on the part of Scott Macmillan who was solely responsible for creating symphonic scores from choral arrangements that made up the repertoire of The Men of the Deeps. Commissioned by Symphony Nova Scotia, Scott even composed a special overture for the opening of the concert: "Pieces of Coal" featured segments of songs from the choir's repertoire.

The concert was a huge success, and was attended by then Nova Scotia Lieutenant Governor Hon. Myra Freeman whose guest, Prince Michael of Kent, she introduced to members of The Men following the performance at Halifax's Rebecca Cohn auditorium. One of the highlights of the concert was The Men of the Deeps tune "Down Among the Coal"[8] which featured tenor Johnny MacLeod (known to the choir members as "Papa John")[9] step dancing to the combined music of Buddy Mac-Master, The Men of the Deeps and Symphony Nova Scotia. Johnny also did that dance routine with Natalie MacMaster when the concert was repeated with the National Arts Centre Orchestra in Ottawa under the direction of David Warrack the following year. (The chorus suffered a great loss when "Papa John" passed away in 2010; his son, John, has now taken on the "step-dancing" role in the group.)

It was also during the concert with Symphony Nova Scotia that a unique element of Scott Macmillan's versatility was showcased. Often when The Men of the Deeps are on tour, local musicians make their way to the dressing rooms to introduce themselves. On one of the choir's previous tours of Western Canada, the group was privileged to meet Kevin Assoun, who asked if he could demonstrate a unique musical instrument that he had constructed. All were amused when his guitar case revealed a pit shovel refashioned into a playable guitar. Needless to say, the instrumentalists in our group were intrigued – particularly the group's lead guitarist at the time, Paul White.

Upon returning home, Paul, being a skillful craftsman in addition to being an excellent guitarist, decided he would try his hand at building his own pit shovel/guitar. Paul's labour was rewarded with success, and when The Men of the Deeps performed with Symphony Nova Scotia at that won-

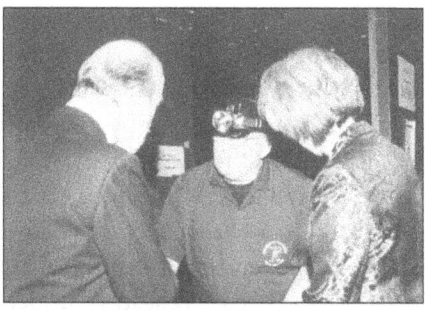

Fig. 6.12 – Prince Michael of Kent (left) and Lt.-Gov. Myra Freeman greet choir member Gordon Sheriff.

Fig. 6.13 – *Chronicle Herald*, n.d. Herald photo by Eric Wynn.

derful concert in March 2002, Paul encouraged conductor Scott Macmillan to show his versatility by "jamming" on Yogi Muise's solo, "Plain Ole Miner Boy." Scott's performance was a hit and evoked a rousing ovation. Thank you to Kevin Assoun for his inspiration.

It is a credit to the arranging skills of Scott Macmillan that those same orchestrations were arranged so that they could be adapted for smaller orchestras as well. This feature allowed the scores to be used when The Men of the Deeps repeated the program at Toronto's Hummingbird Centre with the Canada Pops Orchestra[10] under the direction of David Warrack, and later in Cape Breton with the Cape Breton Chamber orchestra, conducted by Laura Mercer.

The choir came into good fortune in 2003 when Stephen Muise was welcomed into the group as pianist. Stephen is the son of former business manager and long-time member of the bass section, Yogi Muise, and as such, he grew up with the choir. In his early youth he was one of the children who would attend weekly concerts at the Miners' Museum. In 2003 Stephen became actively involved in the production of The Men of the Deeps CD release, *Their Lights Will Shine*, contributing his keyboard talents to the instrumental backup. Stephen has a degree in music from Mount Allison University

Figs. 6.14, 6.15 – In November 2003, a gala dinner for choir director Jack O'Donnell kicked off a national fundraising campaign for the Cape Breton Miners' Museum in Glace Bay.

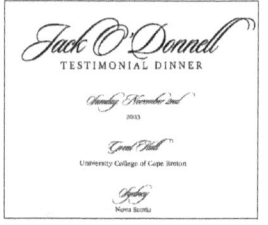

and is now a music educator with the Cape Breton-Victoria Regional School Board. His impressive musical qualifications and unique understanding of the history of the choir, and in particular, his close affiliation with the coal mining communities of Cape Breton, made him an ideal choice for the position of Assistant Musical Director when he officially joined the group in 2006.

Stephen's experience was much like that of Shane MacLeod, currently the electric bass player in The Men of the Deeps band – and son of now deceased founding member, Bob MacLeod. The presence of the sons of some of our long-term singing members gives a new sense of a continuity with regard to the underground traditions that make up the soul of Cape Breton's mining communities. The choir's drummer, Ronnie Leadbeater, is also the son of a coal miner. And rounding out the core of the current band is Kevin Steiger, not only a talented guitarist and singer, but also a person with the necessary qualification of having worked in the mine.[11]

Each recording released has it own special significance. *Their Lights Will Shine* took its title from Ron MacDonald's beautiful tribute to those who perished in the 1992 Westray tragedy. The CD was special to the choir because the cover photo featured a stunning photo of founding member, Bob MacLeod. As has been noted earlier, Bob was a staple of the original "six" which gave birth to The Men of the Deeps; his vocal talents contributed much to the baritone section of the choir until his passing in the year 2000. It is of special significance that Bob's son, Shane, is featured as the soloist on the title song of the CD.

Their Lights Will Shine was the group's first recording with Fred Lavery's Lakewind Sound recording studio. Fred and co-founder of Lakewind, Gordie Sampson, along with recording engineer, Mike Shepherd, produced a quality recording. In addition to the choir's regular band members, the disk featured instrumental backups by some prominent Cape Breton musicians[12]: Fred and Gordie (adding some acoustic guitar); the late Dave McKeough (complementing the electric guitar element); fiddlers, Kyle MacNeil and Kimberly Fraser; and whistles, flute and accordion segments by Stewart MacNeil. (Both Kyle and Stewart are members of the popular Cape Breton group, The Barra MacNeils.)

The "Mining the Soul" tours continued to be extremely popular with audiences and were repeated many times – billed either as simply "Mining the Soul" or, in season, "A Mining the Soul Christmas." Late in 2004, Rita's management began to advertise the show as "Mining the Soul Farewell Tour." No matter how it was billed, the reaction from the press was always favourable: "Down East dynamite," read the London *Free Press* in December 2004; "Very emotional farewell tour brings tears to the eyes," was the comment in the Hamilton *Spectator*; "A cozy Cape Breton Christmas" was proclaimed by the Peterborough *Examiner*; and The Ottawa *Citizen*, picking up on the warmth generated between Rita and the coal miners at Ottawa's Centrepointe Theatre commented, "How deep is your love!"

Much time was devoted to recording and releasing a special 40th-year compact disk in the years 2006 and 2007: *The Men of the Deeps, 40 Years Young* featured a representation of mining songs from the forty-year history of the

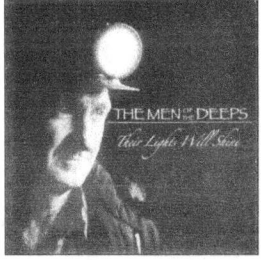

Fig. 6.16 – Their Lights Will Shine, *Men of the Deeps Music, 2004.*

Fig. 6.17 – Poster promoting Rita MacNeil's Christmas 2004 tour, featuring The Men of the Deeps.

Fig. 6.18– Forty Years Young, *Men of the Deeps Music, 2007.*

choir, and like the previous recording produced by Lakewind, graced with the added instrumental talents of Brian Talbot on drums, Colin Grant on fiddle, Fiona MacGillivray on whistle, and with mandolin and guitar additions by Gordie Sampson and Fred Lavery.

When the choir was not in the recording studio, it was pursuing other ways to honour the forty-year milestone. Cape Breton's coal miners choir has always had a history of caring for any segment of society which finds itself in need. Reflecting on this quality, and at the suggestion of the choir's then president, Fred Gillis, The Men of the Deeps decided to honour its fortieth year with a series of concerts to raise funds for Feed Nova Scotia. With the advice and organizational skills of FNS executive director, Dianne Swinemar, a concert tour aimed at reaching small communities throughout the province was christened "Mining for Hope" with the sole aim of raising funds for that worthy cause. In the organization's year-end report, Ms. Swinemar commented:

> I could clearly see why The Men of the Deeps decided to devote their 40th anniversary project to Feed Nova Scotia. Well acquainted with adversity, miners care deeply about the value of community and what it means to look after one another in times of need. These are the values that have made us strong not only in Nova Scotia mining communities, but right across this province. These are values that, in turn, make us strong as Feed Nova Scotia.[13]

Missen Artists Management also kept The Men of the Deeps busy in the mid-part of the decade with major concert tours of Ontario and Western Canada. The western tour in late 2006 began in Kenora, Ontario, and continued west with performances at concert venues in Manitoba, Saskatchewan and Alberta where the group played in Fort MacMurray for the first time – attracting many expat Cape Bretoners who had relocated to Alberta seeking work.

That tour also brought the group to Canada's Northwest Territories for the first time with a concert in Yellowknife and, of particular interest, a concert at the Ekati Diamond Mines – 310 km north of Yellowknife and just 200 km south of the Arctic Circle. Flying out of Yellowknife to the Ekati mine, the choir spent two days at the northern destination. The fact that much of the luggage did not arrive with the group, made for an intriguing venture. The Men had to improvise the mining helmets for the concert: hard hats were borrowed from the diamond miners to which the Men attached a variety of flashlights. With the exception of a tour of the mines, the entire two-day period was spent inside in one large building – apparently because of the abundance of roaming wild bears. Rita's management also kept the men on the go with another "Mining the Soul" tour of Ontario in 2007.

Fig. 6.19 – Lethbridge Herald, *June 19, 2004,* Herald *photo by Rob Olson.*

The year 2008 began with yet another long bus ride! – an 18-hour drive from Cape Breton to Portland, Maine. According to Gurtman and Murtha, The Men of the Deeps, New York management firm, the best connections to Phoenix, Arizona, could be had by flying out of Portland. The Men didn't mind the drive; it just gave them more time to finish their tarabish tournament. (Card games were the favourite pastimes on many long trips.) The group opened the Arizona leg of the tour with a performance in Wickenburg and two shows in Phoenix before flying to Alabama where a performance in Gulf Shores kicked off an extensive tour of Alabama, Florida and the Appalachian areas of Virginia and Kentucky. In some cities the Men gave a matinee as well as an evening concert; the group performed fifteen concerts in two weeks. Since the tour took place during the last week of January and the first week of February, the Men had no complaints about spending six of those days in Alabama and Florida!

Unbeknownst to most members of the group, talent scouts from the international mining equipment giant, Caterpillar, were present in the audience at Sanford, Florida. They were scouting musical talent which might be appropriate for the firm's international conference later in the

Fig. 6.20 – *Poster promoting Rita MacNeil's 2007 Christmas tour featuring The Men of the Deeps.*

Figs. 6.21, 6.22– Programs from concerts in Gulf Shores, Alabama, and Sanford, Florida.

year. As a consequence, The Men soon received an invitation to perform in Las Vegas for a week-long engagement at Caterpillar's global convention extravaganza, MineExpo, in September 2008. The choir performed each night for an international audience; the programs were printed in several languages, including Mandarin. Delegates from China took particular delight at the group's stories recounting the historic trip to China when, as they phrased it (with some awe), "Chairman Mao was still alive!" Surely the fine people whose vision inspired the formation of The Men of the Deeps back in the 1960s could never have envisioned that Cape Breton's coal miners choir would perform for a full week on "The Strip" in Las Vegas.[14]

It was another extraordinarily busy year. Following the inspiring tour of the southern United States and the Appalachian states of Kentucky and Virginia in January and February, and prior to the September Las Vegas experience, the choir was invited to celebrate the 150th anniversary of mining in British Columbia in July and August with an extensive tour of that beautiful province spearheaded and organized by the dynamic mayor of Logan Lake, Ella Brown, and with the backing of British Columbia's giant mining corporation, Tech Cominco.

Before the year was over, Rita MacNeil's "Mining the Soul" tour brought The Men back to Ontario to perform two concerts at Casino Rama.[15] And following those casino shows, Rita continued on her own solo tour while the choir left immediately to visit, for the second time in 2008, the Appalachian

Fig. 6.23 – Collage of post cards and photos of various performances in Las Vegas, Sept. 2008.

mountain area of the United States – this time for performances in Virginia and Pennsylvania.

Coincidentally, this final tour of 2008 coincided with the American election in which Barack Obama was elected president. This was the group's second visit to Big Stone Gap, Virginia – having performed there earlier in the year, during the January/February tour. The sponsors were delighted to have The Men of the Deeps back and arranged for an intimate reception and dinner hosted by a prominent Virginia businessman. Considering that it was the day following the election which elected a Democrat to the White House, The Men found it amusing that the reception was held at a home located on Republican Way!

It would be remembered as a year like no other. But despite the exotic places that hosted the choir's performances (from "The Strip" in Las Vegas to the Ekati Diamond Mines in Canada's Northwest territories to Virginia's Big Stone Gap), one of the most precious memories the men took with them that year was of a special concert in Nova Scotia's Springhill on October 25, when the town commemorated the 50th anniversary of the 1958 "bump" that took seventy-five lives. The concert featured The Men of the Deeps and American folk music legend, Peggy Seeger, along with popular Maritime singer-songwriter, Brian Vartigans.

The busy decade came to a fitting end in 2009 with yet another successful "Mining the Soul Christmas" tour of Central Canada – this time featuring Cape Breton's bluegrass/Celtic/folksinger-song writer and multi-instrumentalist, J. P. Cormier, joining Rita MacNeil and The Men of the Deeps.

Chapter 7

Tha Faileadh a' Ghuail...

Tha faileadh a' ghuail 's an uair air m'aire,
    fhuair mi 'n diugh am Broad Cove.
The scent of the coal I smelled so strongly,
    coming back from Broad Cove.[1]

The extraordinary pace of touring for The Men of the Deeps continued well into the second decade of the new millennium. Having completed an extensive "Mining the Soul Christmas" tour with Rita MacNeil in November and December of 2009 (which took the group from Prince George, British Columbia, to Hamilton Place in Ontario), and following the normal flow of weekly rehearsals throughout January, February and March of 2010, the men were off again – this time on their own – first on a tour of Atlantic Canada, followed immediately with another extensive tour of the province of British Columbia.

Officials at BC's Tech Cominco, following the 2008 tour of that province's celebrations of 150 years of mining, had expressed an interest in bringing The Men of the Deeps back to grace the stages of British Columbia's mining communities once again, fulfilled May 2010. And certainly one of the most interesting concert venues on that tour was a performance at the Britannia Mine Museum, a vibrant, internationally recognized education and tourist destination located between Vancouver and Whistler on the Sea-to-Sky highway. It is a National Historic Site and a BC Historic Landmark. Established in 1974, the site celebrates the contributions of mining and minerals to society, the history of the storied Britannia Beach community and, perhaps more importantly for this century, the ideas and practices of environmental renewal and sustainability.

The performance by The Men of the Deeps was held in the revitalized historic Mill Building – an awe-inspiring cliff-side edifice that has been the symbol of Britannia throughout the years. The performance venue appears to have been carved out of the side of a cliff, and can be seen from miles away on the Sea-to-Sky highway.

That tour prompted the *Canadian Mining Journal* to feature North America's only coal miners choir on the front page of its May 2010 edition. Noting that the choir was scheduled to perform for the potash mining community of Sussex, New Brunswick, upon the group's return to Eastern Canada, the caption read: "Television and Concert personalities, The Men of the Deeps truly serve to illustrate the types of individual it takes to work the coal and potash mines of Canada."[2]

Fig. 7.1 – Canadian Mining Journal, *May 2010.*

The Men have been privileged over the years to sing for many commemorative celebrations honouring the mining industry. The yearly appearances at Davis Day ceremonies in the various towns which make up the greater industrial Cape Breton communities are a good example. But the group has also had the honour of singing the praises of those who have devoted their lives to the mining industry at commemorative services at locations throughout Canada. Gatherings at Springhill and in Plymouth, Nova Scotia, as well as the celebrations honouring British Columbia's coal mining history in 2008 are examples of the outward reach of North America's only coal miners choir.

The membership of the chorus has traditionally been drawn from the industrial Cape Breton communities of Sydney, Glace Bay, New Waterford and Dominion. The distance of travel required for attendance at rehearsals, which are held almost weekly at The Cape Breton

Miners' Museum in Glace Bay, has been a deterrent to potential singers who mined the seams in Cape Breton's Inverness and Victoria Counties on the west coast of the island. The communities of Sydney Mines, Mabou, Broad Cove and Port Hood also have a rich mining tradition and have produced extraordinary musical talent that is known around the world. Mabou's Rankin Family and the popular Barra MacNeils from Sydney Mines are but two examples along with singer/songwriter Bruce Guthro whose song "Men of the Deep," written as a tribute to his father who worked the slopes of Sydney Mines, is a staple of The Men of the Deeps' repertoire.

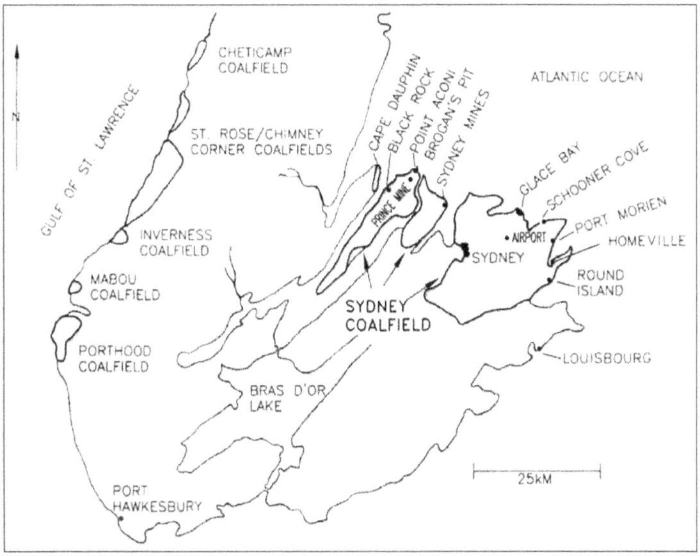

Fig. 7.2 – Map of major coal seams exploited on Cape Breton Island. From An Amateurs Guide to Coal-Plant Fossils on Cape Breton Island, CBU Press 2001.

There is a lovely traditional Gaelic song which originated in the community of Broad Cove that illustrates an early awareness of pollution of the natural environment when coal mining was introduced to the largely farming area in the 18th century. Credited to Alexander MacDonald, the song, which, in translation, begins: "The scent of the coal I smelled so strongly, coming back from Broad Cove," goes on to include a verse quite critical of the invasion of industry into the largely farming area:

Tha 'n gual am Broad Cove
'Na loid g'a tharruinn
Gu bord na luingeas thar chuainn
S' an gearran dubh iarainn,
Is sgiamh 'na anail,
Riasladh fearainn bho luach.

The coal in Broad Cove
In loads is carried
To ships that sail out to sea;
The horse of black iron,
Breath now shrieking,
Is spoiling the farms of their worth.[3]

Fig. 7.3 – Partial score of "Tha Faileadh a' Ghuail," from And Now the Fields are Green, op. cit.

THE SCENT OF THE COAL

73

In July 2011, in celebration of the 225th anniversary of the founding of Port Hood, the choir was invited to participate in the dedication of a Miners Memorial in Port Hood on George's Bay. It was a moving ceremony honouring coal miners who lost their lives in the mines of Inverness County.

The coal seams in the Cape Breton coalfields were formed in a wetland environment dominated by lakes and rivers, not unlike that at Joggins on the mainland of Nova Scotia. A river meandered over the plain depositing layers of sand and mud. Swampy areas clung to its banks, with open lakes on the flood plain. In the swampy areas, plant life flourished. With time, the sand and mud formed the present day sandstones and mudstones or shales. In the swampy areas associated with lakes, peat and plant debris accumulated and were preserved and buried to become the coal seams and black mudstones of today. The coal-bearing rocks of Port Hood have yielded the skeleton of one of the oldest known reptiles, rivalling those found at Joggins on the Nova Scotia mainland.

Fig. 7.4 – Miners Memorial, Ports Hood beach, Port Hood, NS, including an inscription of lines from an Al Prevoe poem.

The last operating mine at Port Hood closed in 1966 – coincidentally, the year of the birth of The Men of the Deeps – and forty-five years later the community saw fit to dedicate a monument to those who gave their lives in the Port Hood coalfield and who are buried in the local churchyard. Cape Breton's past reveals a continuous influx of immigrants from industrial centres all over the world, and among those remembered at the ceremony in Port Hood on July 28, 2011, were four immigrant mine workers from Bulgaria.[4] Their contribution will forever be remembered at the memorial site overlooking the beautiful Port Hood Beach.

The remembrance occasion concluded with a performance by The Men of the Deeps at Strathspey Place located in the heart of Cape Breton's stunning Inverness County – home, of course, to the coalfields surrounding Port Hood, Mabou and Broad Cove.

It was stated earlier in this publication that a particular passion of Cape Breton's coal miners choir has always been to share the stage with some of the burgeoning singers of Nova Scotia's youth choirs. Throughout the previous decade The Men of the Deeps had performed occasionally with the delightful and talented Halifax Boys' Honour Choir, conducted by Pamela Burton;

and like those wonderful occasions with the youth in China and Kosovo and also with the 2006 Red Cross fundraiser "Light the Darkness" concerts, the combination of young singers with Cape Breton's coal miners choir was always a special treat for audience and singers alike. So it was with great anticipation and pride that The Men accepted an invitation to share the stage once again with the talented young singers who make up the Halifax Boys' Honour Choir when the group celebrated its twenty-fifth anniversary year. That concert took place at the Bella Rose Centre in Halifax on March 5, 2011.

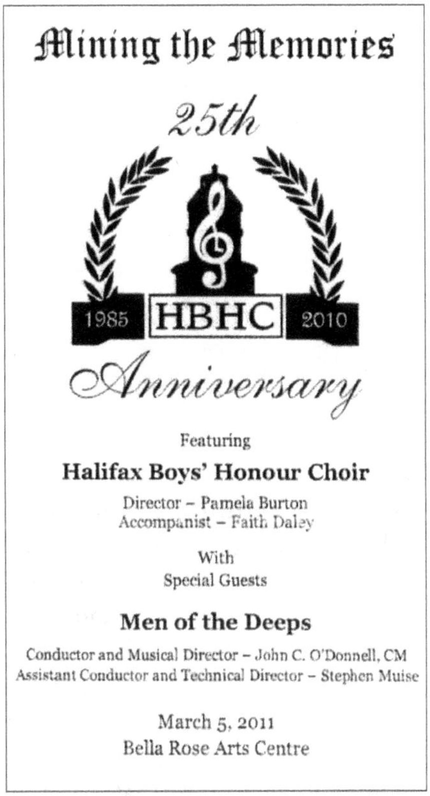
Mining the Memories

25th

1985 HBHC 2010

Anniversary

Featuring

Halifax Boys' Honour Choir

Director – Pamela Burton
Accompanist – Faith Daley

With
Special Guests

Men of the Deeps

Conductor and Musical Director – John C. O'Donnell, CM
Assistant Conductor and Technical Director – Stephen Muise

March 5, 2011
Bella Rose Arts Centre

Fig. 7.5 – Program from 2011 concert with the Halifax Boys' Honour Chioir.

Throughout the past fifty years, The Men of the Deeps choir has been privileged to have had the support and encouragement of a host of successful Cape Breton politicians, television personalities and influential business figureheads. Senator Al Graham, Ann Terry MacLellan and Harvey Webber have already been mentioned within these pages. And holding a special place of honour among that list is businessman Joe Shannon.

Joe Shannon, president of Atlantic Corporation, has worn many hats throughout his years. In the 1980s he reorganized DEVCO, the crown corporation that had been introduced in 1967 to turn the Cape Breton economy around. It was during Joe's tenure as President of DEVCO in the 1980s that the crown corporation turned its first operating profit ever. And it was Joe Shannon who, as Chancellor of Cape Breton University in 1993, conferred the honorary degree Doctor of Letters upon the conductor and musical director of The Men of the Deeps. On May 1, 2012, Joe was made a Companion of the Canadian Business Hall of Fame, and to celebrate the occasion at the Toronto induction ceremony, Joe requested two of his favourite Cape Breton groups: The Barra MacNeils and The Men of the Deeps.[5]

The world-class Celtic Colours International Festival has included performances by The Men of the Deeps most years since it was founded in 1997. Founded to expose the world to the rich Celtic heritage that permeates Cape Breton's musical community, the festival also promotes the wide variety of

Cape Breton talent hailing from the various ethnic and cultural communities that dominate the island. Concerts are held in venues throughout the island, giving visitors and tourists ample opportunity to explore and enjoy not only the colours of Cape Breton's beautiful fall season, but also to absorb the interesting variety of cultures that inhabit this small island.

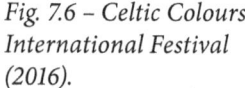

Fig. 7.6 – Celtic Colours International Festival (2016).

Fig. 7.7 – Songs of Steel, Coal and Protest, CD, Centre for Cape Breton Studies, 2015.

The island also boasts a unique educational institution. Cape Breton University offers valuable and insightful courses exploring the cultural mosaic of the island, and the organizers of the Celtic Colours International Festival do not overlook this reality. Celtic Colours appearances of The Men of the Deeps are often paired with musicians or groups that have been supported or promoted because of their attachment to the grass roots of Cape Breton's population resulting in an evening that is educational as well as entertaining. On October 9, 2012, for example, the theme for the evening was "Songs of Work and Protest" based on a project co-produced by Cape Breton University folklore professor Richard MacKinnon. Joining The Men were a host of local, national and international performers whose specialty was in some way representative of the music that has inspired labour movements in Cape Breton and around the world.

Figs. 7.8, Fig. 7.9 – Rita MacNeil's death in 2013 was met with an outpouring of affection. Cape Breton Post, *April 23, 2013.*

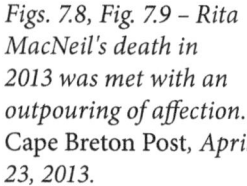

The Men of the Deeps' friend and fellow performer, Rita MacNeil, left this world on April 16, 2013, and in true Rita wit, her instructions were that her ashes be placed in a teapot – "two, if necessary!" She was, indeed, a very special person, and the membership of The Men will be ever grateful for the opportunity she provided for the choir to travel and perform with such a genuine and talented class act. Members of the choir were particularly fortunate to have met many of Rita's admiring public as the they traversed the country, particularly on the popular "Mining the Soul" tours. Many sported pins with Rita's photo proclaiming that they were a member of the Rita MacNeil fan club. And many, of course, included The Men of the Deeps in their rosters of favourite performers.

One of those fans, a particular favourite of Rita's, was Adrian Goderre who accompanied his sister, Shirl Boughner, to many of our Ontario performances, Adrian inevitably came to the concerts laden with small token gifts for Rita, her band and the entire complement of The Men of the Deeps.[6] And now, with Rita gone, Adrian continues to be a loyal fan of the choir.

It was appropriate that the first concert to pay tribute to Rita and her legacy following her passing was organized and planned by her long-time friend and colleague, Scott Macmillan. And it was appropriate that the concert, "Flying on Your Own: A Tribute to Rita MacNeil" took place on March 8, 2014 – the anniversary of her final public performance which, incidentally, was also International Women's Day – a fitting reminder of Rita's devotion to the women's rights movement. Scott conducted Symphony Nova Scotia at the Rebecca Cohn Auditorium in Halifax in a two-hour tribute to Rita featuring some of her most beloved songs performed by Rita's niece, Katriona MacNeil, along with Lucy MacNeil (of the Barra MacNeils) and The Men of the Deeps.

As the choir has done many times throughout its fifty-year history, The Men of the Deeps continued to perform for some worthy fundraising causes in anticipation of the group's 50th-anniversary year. In 2013 it was St. Mary's Polish Parish in Whitney Pier and St. Patrick's Church in Halifax that

Fig. 7.10 – Adrian Goderre, a big fan of Rita MacNeil and The Men of the Deeps, pictured here with Stephen Muise.

Fig. 7.11 – Cape Breton Post, April 18, 2013.

Fig. 7.12 – Poster promoting Concert for St. Mary's Polish Church in Sydney, NS.

were the focus of the year's outreach. The year 2013 came to a conclusion with a cabaret-style concert at the Halifax Forum. It was a surprise to the men, when arriving in Halifax for that Forum concert, to discover several street-side billboards featuring a photo of the group – certainly a first for the coal miners choir.

A particular special friend of the choir, Joe White, celebrated his sixtieth birthday in April 2014. To honour Joe's special birthday, The Men of the Deeps had been asked to make a short video offering congratulations. It was a task that the group readily agreed to, and so arrangements were made to conclude one of the regular Sunday rehearsal sessions with greetings and a couple of songs as a tribute to Joe. The video was later shown on a large screen for Joe and the many friends who gathered to honour his birthday celebration in Antigonish.

Fig. 7.13 (Above) – Halifax billboard publicizing a local concert.

Fig. 7.14 (Right) – L'Arche Antigonish residents Joe White, Don MacIntosh and Joe MacPherson with members of the choir.

Joe, like Rita MacNeil's admiring fan Adrian Goderre, was born with Down Syndrome and is a long-term resident of the L'Arche Community in Antigonish; in fact, he was a founding member of that community which is now in its fortieth year. Joe and his friends in the Antigonish Community have had a close bond with The Men of the Deeps for most of the past forty years. It is because of this bond that members of the choir have grown to know and appreciate the broader community of L'Arche. Founded in 1963 by Jean Vanier, son of former Governor General Georges P. Vanier and Pauline Vanier, L'Arche is an international not-for-profit federation dedicated to the creation and growth of homes, programs and support networks with people who have intellectual disabilities. With more than 150 communities (i.e., clusters of homes, workshops and other facilities) in forty countries around the world, L'Arche brings together people with and without visible disabilities to build communities where the gifts and contribution of every person can be recognized and valued, and where everyone is supported to find a place of belonging.[7]

Largely because of the friendship of Joe and his friends at the community of L'Arche Antigonish, it has not been unusual for members of L'Arche communities across the country to frequent concerts by The Men of the Deeps when the choir performs nearby. The choir was privileged to perform for Jean Vanier at a gathering when he visited Glace Bay in 1988; and on one somewhat tiring concert tour of Ontario in the mid-1990s, the group was feted and performed at a luncheon at Toronto's "Daybreak" community.[8] In October 2014 the choir was asked to participate in the Atlantic Region's festivities celebrating the 50th anniversary of L'Arche International. That concert, which also featured well-known Nova Scotia singer Terry Kelly, took place at the Spatz Theatre in Halifax; as a tribute to Joe White's long friendship with the choir, he was invited to the stage to join in singing the chorus of the closing song – Joe's favourite – Rita MacNeil's "Working Man."

Long-time friend, Senator Al Graham, passed away in April 2014 – a major loss for Canada and for his home province of Nova Scotia. Throughout the choir's fifty years, The Men of the Deeps have benefitted much from Senator Graham's loyalty; from those earliest years when as secretary of the newly formed Cape Breton Development Corporation he so willingly championed the choir's needs for government support, to his later years as senator, his confidence in The Men never faltered. Al's interest in Cape Breton's coal miners choir was driven by his own philosophy that he believed in the ability of the "little guy" to affect change. It will come as no surprise that, following his retirement from the Senate, Al Graham was the first National Patron and Ambassador for L'Arche Canada – a position which he considered one of his most meaningful lifetime responsibilities.

Senator Bernard Alasdair Graham

"Dad. Grampi. Rock. Big Al."

1929-2015

Fig. 7.15

It has always meant much to the membership of The Men of the Deeps to be recognized and appreciated at home, so it was especially meaningful when, as the choir approached its 50th-year anniversary, the Cape Breton Regional Municipality presented The Men with its Ambassadors of the Year Award. That ceremony took place on October 27, 2014, at a special banquet hosted by the Sydney and Area Chamber of Commerce Excellence in Business Awards.

As the year 2015 drew to a close and the choir prepared to celebrate its fiftieth-anniversary year, the men were rewarded on August 30 with an engagement at a very special performance venue. Not that the year's busy schedule wasn't full enough with the usual but always enjoyable summer concert series at Glace Bay's Miners' Museum, Louisbourg's always popular concert series at its unique playhouse, a joint concert with The Cape Breton Chordsmen at the Savoy Theatre, and scattered performances in Heatherton, Pictou, St. Peter's, Bridgewater and Sydney Mines; but a particular compliment was bestowed on The Men of the Deeps when the choir was invited to perform at Prince Edward Island's very successful Indian River Festival in August.

Held annually since 1987, the festival venue, a former Roman Catholic church, is coveted by musicians around the world for its excellent acoustic qualities. The church, now owned by the Indian River Festival Association, is a fine example of the French Gothic influence and was built in 1902 by Island architect, William Critchlow Harris. The Harris trademark, a rib-vaulted or groined ceiling, enhances the quality of sound and archives with the use of fir, pine, spruce, maple and birch throughout the building. Today, St. Mary's remains the architectural and acoustical treasure that Harris envisioned; the perfect setting for voice and instruments to celebrate wonderful music. It has been said that the natural acoustics of St. Mary's rates as one of the top ten places to perform in the world.[9] The Men of the Deeps performance there in the summer of 2015 was a huge success and prompted the organizers of the festival to invite North America's only coal miners choir to return to St. Mary's Church and the Indian River Festival in 2016 as an integral part of the 50th-anniversary year celebrations.

Before the year 2015 came to an end, the choir was privileged to have been asked by opera singer Lorna MacDonald to perform with her at a special concert to be held in her hometown of Port Morien (the birthplace of the coal mining industry in North America). The concert, in her words, was an opportunity "to give back to the community and church that helped to shape her career."[10] The concert, which took place on October 25 in St. John's United Church, was a wonderful success and, needless to say, the men were delighted to share the stage with such a gifted daughter of Port Morien, Cape Breton.

As was the custom for most of the past fifty years, 2015 ended with a series of informal performances celebrating the Christmas Season, at the various nursing homes and senior citizen residences located throughout the Industrial Cape Breton communities of Glace Bay, New Waterford, Dominion, Sydney, Sydney River and Sydney Mines.

Fig. 7.16 – Program from St. John's United Church, Port Morien, concert with Lorna MacDonald.

Epilogue

Throughout these pages I have attempted to reveal the personality of a unique group of men who, in the opinion of many, have done Canada proud. Their dedication, sincerity, camaraderie and genuine Cape Breton wholesomeness have brought laughter and joy to thousands of concert goers on three continents. It is my hope that this publication has introduced the reader to the personality of *the men who work deep in the dark* – individually and collectively.

> **The Men of the Deeps know pain, joy whereof they sing**
> For half a century, this legendary chorus has shared harmonies that light up the dark

Fig. 8.1 – Chronicle Herald, *May 2, 2015.*

In the prologue I paid tribute to three founding members who, in my opinion, represent the heart and soul of The Men of the Deeps. But there are many of whom similar could be said. The list of members (see appendix 2) contains the names of more than 100 individuals who have contributed their vocal and instrumental talents to the choir since its founding in 1966. Some of them you have met in the previous pages, like our longest serving business manager, Yogi Muise (and those who succeeded him in that position, John MacLeod, Jr. and Yogi's son, Stephen) and our longest serving financial manager – whether in his role as secretary or treasurer – Gordon Sheriff[1] and his successor, Kevin Steiger. Their roles have been, and are, vital to the success of the group. Gordon has served on the executive since 1973, having recently been elected to serve as president of The Men of the Deeps.

I think often of founding member Murray Graham who, despite his extraordinary musical talent, insisted on having the musical score in front of him at all times. And if it was an outdoor venue, that music would have to be held with clothes pins on a stand in front of him. For many years Murray was the backbone of The Men of the Deeps instrumental accompaniment and possessed a spirit of generosity and humility that has been the hallmark of many in the group. Murray passed away on March 18, 1997.

Big Jim MacLellan's comic contributions deserve special mention. It's his carefully chosen stories expressing the lighter side of life in a mining community that have brought that necessary levity to the roller coaster of emotions that shine through every concert by The Men of the Deeps.

And I think of Angus MacDonald, one of the several men who have served as president of The Men of the Deeps. Angus loved the group so much that he made a valiant effort to complete one more concert tour with the choir (to Newfoundland) before his cancer took his life.

There are many others, some who have passed on, too numerous to single out here. Throughout the past fifty years, more than one hundred singers have graced concert halls across this continent and beyond with their presence as members of the choir. Some have been mentioned in the preceding chapters, but all enjoy the distinction of having contributed to the success of Cape Breton's coal miners choir.

Nor should the sacrifice of the wives and families of The Men of the Deeps be overlooked. They, in no small measure, have contributed quantitatively to the success of the choir throughout the past fifty years.

The aura of camaraderie which the choir members exude, whether on or off the stage, has certainly been aided by the family connections which have been a part of the group since its inception in 1966 – today's membership being no exception: brothers Nipper and John MacLeod, both first tenors, stand proudly in the front row of the choir formation – and until only a few years ago, their father, "Papa John," also occupied a place in that front row; cousin Mickey MacIntyre, also in the first tenor section, rounds out that "family" group.

Bass player, Shane MacLeod, shares the stage with cousin, Gordon Sheriff; and of course, long-time member Yogi Muise shares the stage with his son, assistant director Stephen Muise.

An examination of the membership lists in the appendix will reveal many more family connections: father and son team, Mickey and Dave Colson are now both deceased. Current member Gerald Burke at one time shared the stage with brother Joe and Joe's son, Robert. Shane MacLeod's dad, Bob (one of the "original six") and uncle Alex were faithful former members. Current member Ray Holland at one time shared the stage with his now deceased cousin, lead guitarist Murray Graham.

Over the years the choir also benefited from the special camaraderie of brothers Francis and Godfry Delaney, Ike and Reg Lambert, Art and Aubrey Martell, and the inseparable brothers Tommy and Eddie Tighe.

The choir owes much to the songwriters whose music has made up the repertoire of The Men of the Deeps; there are well over 100 songs – traditional and newly composed – which I had the privilege of arranging for male choir, an experience I might never have had if it were not for my long involvement with this special breed of men. I am grateful that many of those songs have been preserved on The Men of the Deeps collection of recordings.[2]

Not the least of those songwriters is, of course, Allister MacGillivray, whose songs "The No. 26 Mine Disaster," "Coal Town Road" and his popular ballads praising the beauties of Cape Breton Island have a permanent place in the repertoire of The Men of the Deeps. And his two publications documenting the twenty-five and thirty-five year histories of the choir are necessary reading for anyone interested in the historical significance of the group.

Numerous accolades and honours have been bestowed upon The Men of the Deeps over the past fifty years, and I am humbled to say that some of those honours have spilled over to me: my 1983 induction into the Order of Canada, the various medals in recognition of my service to the country, the honorary degree from Cape Breton University in 1993, the Testimonial Banquet at CBU spearheaded by long-time supporters of The Men of the Deeps like Gus MacMullin and Harvey Webber and hosted by my long-time friend, Charles Keating – and most recently the Dr. Helen Creighton Lifetime Achievement Award – all of which would never have come my way were it not for the unique group of men I have been privileged to have joined me in my career journey.

With the possible exception of the Dr. Helen Creighton Lifetime Achievement Award received during the East Coast Music Week festivities in April 2016, of all the recognition that has come my way over the years, none is more precious to me than the honour I received in September 2013 from Cape Breton University's Beaton Institute and the Fortress Louisbourg.

In 2013 The Katharine McLennan Award was established by Cape Breton University's Beaton Institute and Fortress Louisbourg to recognize the exceptional contributions of an individual who has, through community, life and volunteer work, made a significant and lasting difference to the arts, culture or historical preservation of Cape Breton Island. Katharine McLennan was well-known across Cape Breton Island for her dedication and work toward many causes which supported community and the preservation of history. It was she, along with her father, Senator J. S. McLennan, who strongly advocated for the designation of Fortress Louisbourg as a National Historic Site. I was honoured to be named the inaugural recipient of that award. I will always be grateful to have been a small part of the legacy of North America's only coal miners choir.

J.C.O'D.

Appendix 1

Meet The Men of the Deeps – 2016

Anthony Aucoin

Tony was a miner for twenty-four years. He started at Lingan Colliery and then moved to Phalen and Prince mines. Tony began as a basic labourer and moved on to become a mechanic, working on "anything that moves." He is a fourth-generation coal miner (his brothers, father, grandfathers and great-grandfather all worked in the mines). Tony is a talented songwriter ("A Miner and a Miner's Son," "Let's Go Working in a Coal Mine") and soloist ("Schooldays End"). He is a second tenor and a backup guitarist with the choir.

Jack Beaton

A descendant of the Beatons of Mabou Coal Mines, Jack was offered work in the mines when he was twenty-five years old. He and his wife Charlotte had one child, Jacqueline, and in order to stay in Cape Breton, he took the job. Jack worked at various tasks in three collieries until the government shut down the mines in 2001; he was forty-seven years of age and had nearly twenty-three years of service. Jack received a severance package, but he says it was not the ending he wanted. He is a valuable member of the baritone section and also possesses a fine solo voice.

Bobby Burke

In 1972, at the age of eighteen Bob started working in No. 12 colliery. He worked for DEVCO for four years as an electrician in No. 12 and Lingan Collieries; his father also worked in No. 12 at that time. Bob was working the night that No. 12 colliery caught fire resulting in the loss of two lives and the closing of that mine (refer to Chapter 3). Bob joined The Men of the Deeps in 2015 and is a welcome addition to the baritone section.

Kevin Edwards

Kevin's almost 25-year span with the Cape Breton Development Corporation began at Glace Bay's No. 26 colliery in 1977 at the age of 21 as an underground electrician. In 1980 he was involved with the installation of a groundbreaking Remote Monitoring System, the first in North America. From 1982 until the closing of the last mine in 2001, he worked as an electrical/mechanical/mining and civil draftsman for the corporation. He worked onsite for several years at both the Phalen and Prince collieries, the latter until it closed – which marked the end of coal mining in Cape Breton. Kevin is a fine soloist ("The Ballad of Springhill," "The Ballad of J. B. McLachlan," "The Coal by the Sea" and others); he is a valuable contribution to the baritone section.

Bruce Gillis

Bruce manages The Men of the Deeps website, menofthedeeps.com. He began working as an electrician at Lingan mine in October of 1977 at the age of twenty-four. Bruce began by retrieving the electrical gear from the old levels and then joined the construction crew working out of the shop on the surface. When Lingan closed he was transferred to the Phalen mine and then to Prince mine until it was finally closed in 2001. Over the years he made some very good friends and feels it was an experience that he wouldn't trade for the world. Bruce joined The Men of the Deeps in 2010 and is a valuable member of the baritone section of the choir.

Gerald Burke

Gerald had been employed in mining since January 17, 1955, and worked at all types of jobs in collieries 18, 12, 26 and Lingan. Always conscious of the dangers of working underground, Gerald says when fear comes to your mind, you try to think of something else to chase the thought away, because down in the mine you will have to keep your mind on what you're doing or an accident will happen. Gerald has been a valued member of the baritone section since joining the choir in 1985.

Matt Hawley

Matt started working in the mines in 1974; in both Lingan Colliery and Prince Mine; Matt "did just about everything that there was to do in a mine." Though well experienced on the wall-face, he finished up on the hoist on the surface. Health problems forced him out of the workplace in

1992. Matt is a fine soloist ("Working at the Coalface," "White Christmas") and is a valuable contribution to the second tenor section; when required, he plays both bass and guitar with the group.

Ray Holland

Ray began working in No. 20 colliery in 1953 where he drove a horse. He later loaded coal on the long wall at No. 16. Joining the military in 1956, he returned to the mines in 1963 and began work at No. 20 Colliery until it closed in 1970, at which time he was transferred to DEVCO's central shops as a repairman. From September 1974 to July 1983, Ray worked for the union before returning to the central shops. In the early 1990s he served two terms as President of District 26, UMWA. Ray has written songs for The Men of the Deeps ("The Cape Breton Coal Miners," "No. 26 One Million Ton," "Coal is King Again"). A valuable member of the bass section, Ray is an outstanding soloist. His "signature" song, "Sixteen Tons," regularly brings a standing ovation from the audience.

Carmen Hughes

Carmen started in the millwright course in 1971 and worked as a mechanic in the deeps for roughly ten to fifteen years, during which time he also worked on belt lines. In the mid 1980s he worked as a mine examiner shot firer, shooting down coal and stone with caps and powder where needed. Carmen received his supervisors papers in 1990, and for ten years he worked mostly as a mine examiner checking for methane gas and other safety issues. Like so many of the men in the choir, Carmen says his experience in the mines was a very rewarding one; the friendships and camaraderie experienced under some trying times lasted a lifetime. Since joining the group in 2007, Carmen has been a valued member of the baritone section.

Jude Kelly

Jude began working underground in the coal mines at the age of eighteen. During a period of eleven years, he worked in four different mines in various capacities including a pit-pony driver, an electro/mechanic and a mine electrician. After obtaining mine manager's certification, Jude accepted a position with the Nova Scotia government and spent the last twenty years of his mining career working as an electrical/mechanical and mine's safety inspector for the province of Nova Scotia. Jude is a talented soloist ("Are You From Bevan?," "Down in the Hillcrest Mine," "The Coal by the Sea") and except for the eighteen-year absence when he held down his mine's safety position, he has been a faithful and valuable member of the first tenor section since 1974.

Ernest Kliza

Ernie started working as an electrician in Lingan Mine in 1978, working mostly on the east side wall face. When Lingan closed, he transferred to Phalen Colliery, working electrical; and when Phalen closed he transferred to Prince Colliery brushing west main intake until he transferred back to electrical where he remained until the Cape Breton Development Corporation closed. Ernie is a recent addition to The Men of the Deeps and sings in the baritone section.

Ron Leadbeater

Ron is a valuable member of the The Men of the Deeps band. Having not had the required two years experience working underground in the mines, he is not an official member of the group. But he is an integral part of the unique sound of the group which audiences have come to expect. Ron's family has been involved in the mining industry since the 1800s when his great grandfather, Tom Leadbeater, came over from England, starting in the mines at the age of eight. Ron's grandfather, his father, brother, uncles and cousins, were all coal miners. Ron was the first in his family not to work in the mines. After losing an uncle at the age of twenty-seven in No. 12 colliery, Ron decided to never work as a miner. Ron's uncle, Earl Leadbeater, died in the 1971 fire in New Waterford's No. 12 colliery (see chapter 3). The Men are proud to list Ron Leadbetter as an integral and necessary member of the group.

Mickey MacIntyre

Mickey started working in the mines at age twenty-one, working at Lingan, Phalen and Prince Mines. In his twenty-two years underground, he worked on the wall-face, operated shear jacks and worked as a material man, diesel operator and console operator. As well, Mickey was involved as a draegerman and held several other underground positions. Mickey is a cousin to Nipper and John MacLeod; he is a talented soloist ("A Mining Town No More," "The Men of the Deep," "Coal, Not Dole") and sings with the first tenor section.

Jim MacLellan

Jim spent thirty-nine years in the mines, serving both DOSCO and DEVCO. He started work in 1951 and in 1955 was transferred to the mine engineering department as a surveyor in the New Waterford area. In 1959, he was promoted to the position of Vent engineer for the Cape Breton area. In 1964, he was made field engineer for Cape Breton and part of mainland Nova Scotia. Jim became assistant manager on No. 12 Colliery in 1968, and in 1972 he was named general manager of Glace Bay's No. 26 Colliery; he also served as manager of the Prince Mine. From 1980 to 1982 Jim served as DEVCO's production manager, mechanization manager (1983-89), and for nine months in 1989 he was senior planner. Jim's mining career has seen him work in approximately fifteen Cape Breton mines. In various capacities he has travelled to the U.S., the U.K., Germany, Poland and Russia. "Big Jim" is an original member of The Men of the Deeps; he is the group's stand-up comic, but also uses his talent for speaking by offering interesting historical notes to complement some of the musical arrangements in many concerts.

John MacLeod

John was hired on with DEVCO in 1977 as a journeyman electrician for Lingan Mine; he was twenty-six years old at the time. He worked underground on the production walls and was responsible for maintaining and troubleshooting all electrical equipment in that section. He also worked in the development sections, where the deeps and wallface roadways were driven, installing and maintaining electrical switchgear, fans, belt drives and cutting machines. In October 1989, he was transferred to the Lingan Mine surface electrical shop where he tested and set up switchgear, fans, motors, etc., for installation underground. In January 1992, he transferred to the Prince Mine electrical shop with the same responsibilities as he had at the Lingan Mine. In November 1994 John was elected to a union position with the United Mine Workers of America and served as the international executive board member for District 26, up to February, 2003. John is a brother to Nipper MacLeod and a cousin to Mickey MacIntyre. He sings with the first tenor section and has a talent for step-dancing – inherited from his father, "Papa" John MacLeod.

Nipper MacLeod

Nipper worked underground for twenty years, first at No. 12 colliery (until its closure in 1975) and later at Lingan. Nipper is a brother to John MacLeod and a cousin to Mickey MacIntyre and is a valuable and talented soloist ("Immigrant Eyes," "She Loves Her Miner Lad," "Now that the Work is Done," "Sweet Guinevere," "Song for the Mira," "Working Man" and others). His recording of Rita MacNeil's "Working Man" rivals only that of Rita's own recording of the song. Nipper sings with the first tenor section.

Shane MacLeod

Shane's great-grandfather came from Scotland in 1902 and worked the coal mines on Cape Breton's northside area until he was killed in the Princess Mine in 1912. Shane's grandfather worked at No. 6 mine in Donkin and at No. 4 mine in Caledonia, Glace Bay. Shane, himself, worked for many years in the mine engineering department, working in various aspects of the operation, namely underground construction, ventilation and geology. He has worked at Lingan, and No 26. colliery, and has also been involved in the Donkin-Morien Development Project and the Phalen Mine. He finished his mining career as a development supervisor. In addition to possessing an excellent solo voice ("Farewell to the Rhondda," "She's Called Nova Scotia," "Matthew's Voyage," "Trapper Boy," "If I Can't Take the Island With Me," "Their Lights Will Shine" and more), Shane plays bass guitar with the group and has served several years as president. His father, Bob, was a founding member of The Men of the Deeps and toured with the group for more than thirty years.

Bill MacPherson

In November of 1970, Bill began his mining career as an electrician in Lingan Colliery. Nineteen years later, he transferred to the Victoria Junction wash-plant as a fine-coal operator. In 1998, he retired as an operator at the water-treatment plant. Bill is a second tenor and possesses a fine solo voice ("Coal Town Road," "Dad's Old Dinner Pail," "The Mary Ellen Carter," "Bluenose," "Christmas in the Mine" and others). Bill does an excellent job managing the choir's CD sales.

Jackie MacQueen

Jack is the son of a miner with forty years experience, he was employed with the Cape Breton Development Corporation's railroad for more than twenty years. Starting work with DEVCO in 1978, he remained with the crown corporation until it closed. He stayed on with the company that took over the rail line and finally retired as a locomotive engineer in 2013 after thirty-five years of service. Jack has served several terms on the executive of the choir, and is a valuable soloist ("You'll Be Home Again," "The Chain Runner Song," "Coal, Not Dole," "My Love Cape Breton and Me," "Rise Again").

Alf Matheson

Alf started in the mine at the age of eighteen. His first job was on payroll in the office. (The men were paid by cash in those days.) He eventually moved to underground jobs where the pay was better. Alf's last job was with mine engineering, installing the new coal cutters and walking supports. He spent seventeen years underground and eventually left the mine in 1971. He is a faithful member of the bass section.

Gary Micholsky

Gary returned from work in Ontario in 1975 and worked in Lingan mine as a mechanic. In 1980 he became supervisor of long wall and remained at Lingan Mine for seventeen years, until 1991, when he was transferred to Prince Mine. Twenty-two of the twenty-four years working underground were spent at the coal face. Gary retired in 1999 and had the pleasure of working with many members as miners and now is honoured to sing with them as The Men of The Deeps.

Melvin Mugford

Melvin started in 1970 right out of high school at eighteen years old. He took a four-year industrial mechanic course through DEVCO and worked the next thirty years at No. 26, the Phalen and Prince mines – twenty-four of those years underground and the last six on the surface until DEVCO shut down – mainly on belt lines, the jacks and machines. He says he is on an early retirement program until he reaches sixty-five and goes on old age pension. Melvin has worked the past years part time as a carpenters helper. He misses all the joking and good times with his buddies in the pit. Melvin is a valuable member of the first tenor section.

Stephen Muise

Since 2006, Stephen has served in the capacity of assistant musical director, technical director and leader of The Men of the Deeps band. Like drummer Ronnie Leadbeater, Stephen is the son of a miner. (His dad, Yogi Muise, is one of the longest serving members of the choir.) In addition to his work with The Men of the Deeps, Stephen is a music educator with the Cape Breton-Victoria Regional School Board, and he has performed with many well-known Cape Breton musicians such as The Rankin Family, Bruce Guthro, Matt Minglewood and the late Rita MacNeil. He holds a degree in music from Mount Allison University. As The Men of the Deeps celebrate the choir's 50th-year anniversary, Stephen is poised to assume the responsibilities of full-time conductor and musical director of the chorus.

Yogi Muise

Yogi has two years of mining experience, having left the pit to complete an education degree. For many years, he taught geology to students at New Waterford's Breton Education Centre, and he often arranged underground tours for the senior high school students. Yogi was the longest-serving business manager of The Men of the Deeps and plays acoustic guitar and banjo for the group; he is also a fine soloist ("Just A Jolly Miner," "Coal Town Road," "Cape Breton Silver," "I'm Just an Old Chunk of Coal").

Jack O'Donnell

Jack has served as conductor and musical director of The Men of the Deeps for most of the past fifty years. Like Stephen Muise and Ron Leadbeater, he has not had experience working in the underground mines – which is a source of friendly humour and belittlement with the experienced miners who make up the membership of the choir. Jack is Professor

Emeritus at St. Francis Xavier University in Antigonish and holds graduate degrees in music from Gonzaga University in Spokane, Washington, and the University of London King's College in London, England.

John Prendergast

In 1972 John started work in the iron foundry, eventually transferring to the pattern shop where he helped to build rakes and everything pit related. John was eventually transferred to the construction crew and worked around every pit including the Donkin mine. He also worked in the Lingan Mine and finished his working career as a stationary engineer in the heating plant. John joined The Men of the Deeps in 2010 and sings in the bass section.

Bob Roper

Bobby began his mining career as an underground worker at No. 12 colliery in 1951, beginning as a chuckdrawer's helper which prepared him for loading coal. In 1952 Bob was buried in the mine, following which he went on compensation for over eleven months. When he was able, he returned to work in the same mine in order to get over his fear. Bob worked in the mines for more than thirty years at Nos. 12, 18, 26 and Lingan collieries. He is one of the original members of The Men of the Deeps and has served well as one of the group's most distinctive soloists ("Billy, Come With Me," "Dark as a Dungeon," "The Lonely Fiddler," "The Ballad of Joe Hill" and more).

Gordon Sheriff

Gordon began his work with the Dominion Coal Company in the railway department in 1964, which brought him to the surface of both No. 20 and No. 26 collieries tabulating the amount of coal loaded. In 1968 he received a DEVCO scholarship and graduated from the University College of Cape Breton (now Cape Breton University) in 1971. He has worked in various departments since graduation, the longest being with the purchasing department; this required him to travel underground to increase his knowledge of the equipment used. Gordon has served on the executive of The Men of the Deeps continually since 1973 and was recently elected president of the choir (replacing Shane MacLeod, in that position). His renditions of some of Al Provoe's poetry ("Who Are They?," "Aftermath") are a particular highlight of many concerts. He is a valuable soloist ("Sea People," "Today We Took a Friend from the Mine," "Coal is King Again," "Away From the Roll of the Sea") and sings with the second tenor section.

Kevin Steiger

Kevin worked worked underground in the Cape Breton coal mines for twenty-five years: at the Lingan Colliery (1976-1991), Phalen Colliery (1991-

1999) and latterly at the Prince Mine (1999-2001). He worked as an electrician, but also had mine examiners papers and supervisors papers which qualified him to handle explosives and to do underground blasting. Those papers also qualified him to supervise working sections and men. Kevin is a fine soloist ("Working at the Coal Face") and plays guitar, mandolin and sometimes, piano with The Men of the Deeps band.

Sen White

Sen worked twenty-one years in the Lingan, Phalen and Princess collieries, starting at thirt-two years of age. He was a conveyor belt mechanic. Sen has served as "disciplinarian" and trip organizer and sings with the bass section of the choir.

Appendix 2
THE MEN OF THE DEEPS: 1966-2016

Membership in 2016	Band in 2016
Tenor 1	Stephen Muise [keyboards]
Judy Kelly (1974-1980, 1998-)	Kevin Steiger [lead guitar, mandolin]
Mickey MacIntyre (1984-)	Shane MacLeod [electric bass]
John MacLeod (2004-)	Ron Leadbeater [drums]
Nipper MacLeod (1976-)	Yogi Muise [banjo, guitar]
Melvin Mugford (1995-)	Bob Roper [harmonica]
	Richard Burke [backup keyboards]
Tenor 2	**Former Musicians**
Tony Aucoin [guitar] (1998-)	David Colson [electric bass] *deceased*
Matt Hawley [guitar] (1998-)	George Demeter [accordion]
Bill MacPherson (1993-)	Rod Elias [guitar]
Jackie MacQueen (1986-)	Murray Graham [guitar] *deceased*
Bob Roper [harmonica] (1966-)	Freddie Hamood [violin] *deceased*
Gordon Sheriff (1968-)	Terry Hill [rehearsal assistant]
Kevin Steiger [guitar, mandolin] (2004-)	Gordon LeDrew [double bass] *deceased*
	Wally MacAulay [guitar, banjo, mandolin]
Baritone	Alex MacDonald [drums]
Jackie Beaton (1994)	Danny MacIntyre [accordion] *deceased*
Bobby Burke (2015-)	Cyril MacNeil [guitar]
Gerald Burke (1985-)	Jimmie MacNeil [piano]
Kevin Edwards (1978-)	Wayne Scheller [electric base] *deceased*
Bruce Gillis (2010-)	Gertie Watts [piano] *deceased*
Carmen Hughes (2007-)	George Webb [piano] *deceased*
Ernie Kliza (2015-)	Paul White [guitar]
Shane MacLeod [electric bass] (1981-)	

Membership cont'd	Musical Directors
Bass	Jack O'Donnell (1966-68, 1973-2015)
Ray Holland (1966-1980, 1994-)	Stephen Muise (asst. dir., 2006-)
Jim MacLellan (1966-1972, 1986-)	Fred Scott (1969-1974)
Alfie Matheson (1995-)	Sister Rita Clare, CND (1969)
Gary Micholsky (2004-)	Aubrey Boone (1968-1969)
Yogi Muise [banjo, guitar] (1969-)	Steve MacGillivray (founding dir., 1966)
John Prendergast (2010-)	
Sen White (2001-)	

Former members	
Joe Burke	Melvin MacKenzie
Robert Burke	Cyril MacNeil [guitar]
Jack Davis	Gerard MacNeil
George Demeter [accordion]	Philip MacNeil
Bernie Edmund	Bill Marsh, Jr.
Wilf Edmund	George Merrill*
Gerry Forbes	Roy Peach
Sid Forgeron	Earl Sampson
Fred Gillis	John Terry [electric bass]
Alex MacDonald [drums]	Paul White [guitar]
Ron MacDonald	

Deceased members	
Richard Burton	Francis MacKenzie
Alex Bezanson	Roy MacLean*
Matt Breski	Alex MacLeod
David Colson [electric bass]	John MacLeod
Mickey Colson	"Papa" John MacLeod
Bill Copland	Bob MacLeod*
Biff Davis	Jimmy P. MacNeil
Francis Delaney	Bert MacPherson
Godfrey Delaney	Art Martell
Shep Doucette	Aubrey Martell
Mike Flemming	Don Matheson
Murray Graham [guitar]	Doug Morris
Gordon Green	Ernie Poirier

Freddy Hamood [violin]	Marshall Poirier
Freeman Jenkins	Al Provoe
Don Kerr	Francis Quan
Ike Lambert	Mose Roberts
Reg Lambert	Wayne Scheller [electric bass]
Gordon Le Drew [double bass]	Charles Sheppard
Leslie Lewis*	Jack Stevens
Angus MacDonald	Bruce Sudworth
Myles MacDonald*	Eddie Tighe
Francis MacIntosh	Tommy Tighe
Dan MacIntyre [accordion]	Bart Watkins
Clark MacKenzie*	Dave Watts
	John Williams
*Original six founding members	

Appendix 3

MAJOR EVENTS, CONCERTS and TOURS

1966-2016

The following highlights major concert events over the past fifty years. It does not include those annual concert obligations that take place on a regular basis (i.e., summer concerts held weekly at the Cape Breton Miners' Museum, Davis Day [June 11] commemoration performances, the Ann Terry MacLellan "Curl for Cancer" bonspiel performances annual Christmas concerts at Industrial Cape Breton hospitals and palliative care homes, annual fall appearances at North Sydney's Farmers' Exhibition, and Louisbourg Playhouse annual summer concert series).

Local mine disasters and the passing of persons who have been friends or mentors to The Men of the Deeps are noted in italics throughout the list.

1966 ·Debut Concerts (Jack O'Donnell, Musical Director)
      Savoy Theatre, Glace Bay (November 1)
      Vogue Theatre, Sydney (November 2)
      Paramount Theatre, New Waterford (November 3)
1967 ·Opening of Cape Breton Miners' Museum, Glace Bay
    ·Expo '67, Montreal
1968 ·Release of first vinyl recording: *The Men of the Deeps* (Apex)
      (Aubrey Boone, Producer & Musical Director)
1969 ·Industrial Cape Breton Concerts (Sister Rita Clare, CND, Musical Director)

1969-1973	·Debut Concerts in Ontario & Western Canada (Fred Scott, Musical Director)
1973	·Tour of Manitoba & Ontario (Fred Scott, Musical Director)
	·*Explosion in No. 12 Colliery – one life lost*
	·Colliery Lands Park created on the site of former No. 12 Colliery.
	·Cape Breton Development Corporation initiates sponsorship of The Men of the Deeps (Jack O'Donnell, Musical Director)
	·Performances: Canadian Music Council & Canadian Folk Music Society (Halifax)
	·Canadian Assoc. of University Schools of Music (Toronto)
1974	·Performance at the Nova Scotia Festival of the Arts (Halifax)
	·Performance at the National Multi-Cultural Folk Festival (Ottawa)
	·Concert tour of Manitoba and Nova Scotia with The Men of the Deeps & Winnipeg's Rusalka Ukrainian Dancers
1975	·Parliament Hill Canada Day Concert
	·Concert at Lester B. Pearson Theatre, Department of External Affairs, Ottawa
	·Concert tour of Northern Manitoba & Nova Scotia (w/ Rusalka Ukrainian Dancers)
	·Release of LP vinyl recording *The Men of the Deeps* (Waterloo)
	·Publication of first songbook: *The Men of the Deeps* (Waterloo)
1976	·Concert Tour of The People's Republic of China (June)
	·Silver Donald Cameron's *Weekend Magazine* diary of the China experience:
	"Behind the Rising Sun" (November 20)
	"Underground in China" (November 27)
	"Marx, Mao and Morality" (December 4)
	"A Tale of Two Chinas" (December 11)
	·Concert appearances at Montreal Summer Olympics (July), Atlantic Folk Festival (August), United Mine Workers of America, Cincinnati, Ohio (September)
1977	·Television appearance: *Ninety Minutes Live* with Peter Gzowski
	·Performances at the International Girl Guide Camp (Mira, Cape Breton), Atlantic Folk Festival (Halifax) and Cape Breton's Tarbot Folk Festival
	·Television appearance: *Front Page Challenge*
	·Release of LP vinyl recording *The Men of the Deeps II* (Waterloo)
1978	·Concert Tour of Nova Scotia
	·Summer Performances aboard the Sydney & Louisbourg Railway
	·Taping of National Film Board vignettes
1979	·Performance aboard luxury liner *QE II*, Sydney Harbour
	·*Explosion in Glace Bay's No. 26 Colliery claims twelve lives* (Feb.)

- *Alan Tighe, son of choir member Tommy Tighe, killed in Lingan Colliery* (July)
- National Film Board feature: *The Nearest Point to Everywhere*
- National Film Board vignette: *The Coal By The Sea*
- Performances at the inaugural *Nova Scotia Tattoo*, Halifax (July) and the United Mine Workers of America, Denver, Colorado (December)

1980
- Concert tour of Labrador and Northern Quebec (December)
- CBC Television Performance: *Canadian Express*

1981
- Television appearance: *Anne Murray Christmas Special* (CTV & CBS)
- Television Performance: *A Christmas Greeting* (CBC)

1982
- Performance at DeCoste Centre for the Performing Arts, Pictou, NS
- Performance at Annapolis Valley Apple Blossom Festival (May)
- CanPro Awards television appearance (CTV)
- Television performance: *Take Thirty* (CBC)

1983
- Order of Canada conferred upon Musical Director, John C. (Jack) O'Donnell
- Performance for Asian Physicists Seminar: Science for Peace (Baddeck, NS)
- Global Television Network "Special"

1984
- Performance at DeCoste Centre for the Performing Arts (Pictou)
- Gala Concert for visiting Tall Ships (Sydney Harbour)
- First appearance with Rita MacNeil: Savoy Theatre, Glace Bay
- Release of LP vinyl recording *The Men of the Deeps III* (Waterloo)

1985
- "Coal Town Jubilee" *Live* on CBC radio from Glace Bay's Savoy Theatre
- *Long-time mentor Ann Terry MacLellan passed away on June 15, 1985*
- Tribute to Terry MacLellan: Men of the Deeps & Rita MacNeil (Savoy Theatre)
- Performances in Liverpool and Pictou, NS

1986
- 20th-Anniversary Year Concert: Rebecca Cohn Auditorium, Halifax (January)
- Performances aboard *QE II*, Sydney (June)
- Sharon Temple Festival in Newmarket, Ontario (July)
- Expo '86, Vancouver (July)
- Victoria International Festival (August)
- American Federation of Musicians, Sydney (August)

1987
- Opening of Centre 200, Sydney (June)

	·Rita MacNeil & The Men of the Deeps: Miramichi Folk Song Festival, Newcastle, New Brunswick (June)
1988	·Closing ceremonies: The World Junior Olympics, Sudbury
1989	·Performances at the Juno Awards, Toronto (March) and the International Choral Festival, Roy Thomson Hall, Toronto (June)

- Opening of the Anne Murray Centre in Springhill (July)
- Television performance: CTV *Live It Up* (November)

1990
- Performances at New Brunswick's Potash mining community of Sussex (March)
- Festival Chanteguay, Chateauguay, Quebec

1991
- *Nina Cohen passed away March 8, 1991 at the age of 84*
- Tourism Industry Association of Nova Scotia Award
- Release of CD, *Diamonds in the Rough* (Men of the Deeps label)
- Publication of Allister MacGillivray's *Diamonds in the Rough, 25 Years with The Men of the Deeps*
- Performances at Centre 200 (Sydney), Shriners' Convention (Sydney), Bras d'Or Festival (Baddeck), Seniors' Expo (Halifax), Prince Edward Island Summer Festival.
- CBC television taping: DeCoste Centre, Pictou

1992
- *Westray Mine Explosion, Plymouth, Nova Scotia, claims 26 lives (May 9)*
- Westray Benefit Concerts in Halifax (May) & Charlottetown, PEI (June)
- Truro, NS and Newcastle NB (May), Antigonish & Dominion (June)
- Halifax: Seniors Expo' (July), Yarmouth: The Y'Arc (August)
- Pictou DeCoste Centre (September)
- New Brunswick Tour (September)
- Springhill (October)
- Publication of John C. O'Donnell's collection of coal mining songs in Canada: *And Now the Fields are Green* (University College of Cape Breton Press)
- Anne Murray television special with guests Rita MacNeil, The Rankin Family, The Gospel Heirs and The Men of the Deeps

1993
- Doctor of Letters, *honoris causa*, bestowed upon John C. O'Donnell, by University College of Cape Breton (now Cape Breton University)
- Performance at DeCoste Entertainment Centre, Pictou (Sept.)

1994
- First appearance at the Elora Festival, Guelph, Ontario.
- "Light the Darkness" fundraising tour of Nova Scotia in aid of the Canadian Red Cross

1995
- Concert performance: Manitouwadge, Ontario

	·"Summit Ceilidh" on Citadel Hill, Halifax to honour G7 Summit held in Halifax in June
	·Performance on *Rita and Friends* television special
	·Release of Compilation CD *Buried Treasures* (Atlantica)
1996	·Second appearance at the Elora Festival, Guelph, Ontario
	·Second "Light Up the Darkness" tour in aid of the Canadian Red Cross
	·Release of CD *Coal Fire in Winter* (Island Recordings)
1997	·Folkorist Edith Fowke passed away March 28, 1996, at the age of 83
	·Concert Tour of Ontario (May)
	·Performance for Jean Vanier L'Arche gathering, Glace Bay (May)
	·"Light Up the Darkness" Red Cross concert (Sydney Mines, May)
	·Algoma Festival (October)
	·*A Celtic Celebration* at Hamilton Place featuring the Bach-Elgar Choir, John Allan Cameron and the family of Stan Rogers
	·Concert tour of Western Canada (October)
1998	·CBC television appearance with Vicki Gabereau (January)
	·Concert tour of Newfoundland (April)
	·Third "Light Up the Darkness" tour in aid of the Canadian Red Cross
	·New Brunswick concert tour (October)
	·Recording: *Awakening* (*Dry Away Your Tears*) with Roger Whitaker (October)
1999	·Granville Green, Port Hawkesbury welcomes Vanessa Redgrave
	·Ontario concert tour (April)
	·Performance of National Anthems at Toronto Blue Jays vs. Anaheim at Toronto's Skydome (now the Rogers Centre)
	·Performance at CBC's Glenn Gould Studio
	·Performance at the British Embassy, Skopje, Macedonia
	·Concert performance at "The Return," Pristina, Kosovo (September)
	·Rita MacNeil & The Men of the Deeps American tour
2000	·Doctor of Letters, *honoris causa*, bestowed upon The Men of the Deeps by University College of Cape Breton (now Cape Breton University)
	·The Men of the Deeps added to the Walk of Stars by Glace Bay's Savoy Theatre
	·Performances in Elliot Lake, Ontario (July)
	·Joint concert with Newfoundland's Folk of the Sea, St. John's (July)
	·Concert tour to Montreal and Ontario (September/October)
	·Performance for St. Francis Xavier University Homecoming
	·Gala Dinner for The Men of the Deeps – Senator Al Graham guest speaker.

	·Publication of Allister MacGillivray's *The Men of the Deeps: The Continuing Saga*
	·Cross-country "Mining the Soul" concert tour (Nov./Dec.)
2001	·Honorary doctoral degree awarded to Vanessa Redgrave by St. Francis Xavier University
	·Performance for Nova Scotia Choral Federation's "Suas e!" summer festival
	·Performances at Timmons, Ontario (August)
	·"Mining the Soul" Ontario tour (November)
	·"Mining the Soul" Tour of Maritime Provinces (December)
2002	·*Long-time mentor, Harvey Webber passed away in January*
	·National Film Board of Canada documentary: *The Men of the Deeps*
	·Symphony Nova Scotia presents The Men of the Deeps and Cape Breton fiddle icon, Buddy MacMaster (Rebecca Cohn Auditorium, Halifax)
	·Concert Tour of Saskatchewan, Albert & Ontario (September)
	·"Mining the Soul Christmas" Cross-Country Tour (November/December)
2003	·Hummingbird Centre, Toronto: The Men of the Deeps and the Canadian Pops Orchestra
	·National Arts Centre, Ottawa: The Men of the Deeps and the National Arts Centre Orchestra
	·Cobequid Education Centre, New Waterford: The Men of the Deeps and the Cape Breton Chamber Orchestra
	·Testimonial Dinner honouring The Men of the Deeps musical director
2004	·*Nicholas Goldschmidt passed away February 8, 2004 at the age 96*
	·*Daniel Petrie succumbed to cancer, August 2004*
	·Release of CD *Their Lights Will Shine* (Lakewind)
	·"Mining the Soul Christmas" concert tour of Ontario
2005	·"Mining the Soul" Maritimes tour
	·*Mining the Soul* television special
2006	·Appearance at Cape Breton's Coal Bowl Tournament (New Waterford)
	·Concert tour of Ontario (April)
	·Savoy Theatre tribute to the memory of Wendy Mulse (May 28)
	·"Mining for Hope" concert tour of Nova Scotia in aid of Feed Nova Scotia (July)
	·Memorial for Ken Thomson: Roy Thomson Hall, Toronto (Sept.)
	·Concert tour of Western Canada including performances in Yellowknife and the Ekati Diamond Mine in Canada's Northwest Territories (October)

2007	·Savoy Theatre with Cape Breton Chamber Orchestra (May)
	·Celtic Colours, Sydney (October), DeCoste Centre (October)
	·Release of CD *Forty-Years Young* (Lakewind)
	·"Mining the Soul" concert tour of Ontario (November)
2008	·Concert tour of Arizona, Alabama, Florida and the Appalachian Mountain areas of Virginia and Kentucky (January/February)
	·Give St. Patrick a Hand concert, Halifax (March)
	·*Folklorist Archie Green, widely considered the dean of coal mining music scholarship, passed away on March 22 at the age of 91*
	·*Friend & entertainer John Allan Cameron passed away on April 3 at age 67*
	·Concert tour of British Columbia celebrating 150 years of mining in that Province (July/August)
	·Mine Expo concerts in Las Vegas, Nevada (September)
	·Casino Rama concert with Rita MacNeil & The Men of the Deeps (October)
	·Concert tour of Virginia and Pennsylvania (November)
	·"Mining the Soul Christmas" tour of Central Canada
2009	·Publication: *The Music of The Men of the Deeps* (Amberglade)
	·"Mining the Soul Christmas" tour of Western & Central Canada
2010	·Concert Tour of Atlantic Canada
	·Concert Tour of British Columbia
2011	·Celebration of the 225th anniversary of the founding of Port Hood: Performance at dedication of Miners Memorial & performance at Strathspey Place, Mabou
	·Performance to honour Halifax Boys Honour Choir 25th Anniversary (Halifax: Bella Rose Centre)
2012	·Concert Tour of Ontario (March)
	·Performance at Celtic Colours: "Songs of Protest" (October)
	·Joe Shannon inducted in the Canadian Business Hall of Fame (Toronto), Performance by The Men of the Deeps & The Barra MacNeils
2013	·*Fellow performer Rita MacNeil passed away April 1, 2013 at the age of 68*
	·Performance honouring the 100th anniversary of St. Mary's Polish Parish (Sydney)
	·Katharine McLennan Award ceremony & concert, Louisbourg (September)
	·"Ha-Ha-Holidaze" performance, Savoy Theatre (December)
2014	·Tribute to the late Rita MacNeil at Rebecca Cohn Auditorium, Halifax (May)

- Performance commemorating the 50th anniversary of L'Arche International, Spatz Theatre, Halifax (October)
- "Ha-Ha-Holidaze" performance, Savoy Theatre (December)

2015
- *Good friend Senator Al Graham passed away on April 22 at the age of 85*
- Commemoration of 90th year commemoration of Davis Day, New Waterford
- Performances at Prince Edward Island's Indian River Festival (Aug.)
- Performance with Lorna MacDonald honouring town of Donkin, the birthplace of coal mining in North America
- Cape Breton Regional Municipality Ambassadors of the Year award (October)
- "Ha-Ha-Holidaze" performance, Savoy Theatre (December)

2016
- Concert Tour of Ontario (April)
- Jack O'Donnell awarded the Dr. Helen Creighton Lifetime Achievement Award (April)
- Release of 50th Anniversary Year Compilation CD, *Coal to Gold*
- Gala concerts celebrating The Men of the Deeps @ 50 (April/May)
- Tour of Atlantic Provinces, Nov 1 - 9.
- 50th-Anniversary celebration of The Men of the Deeps, November 1, 2016
- 50th-year publication: *The Men of the Deeps: A Journey with North America's Only Coal Miners Chorus*

APPENDIX 4

The Repertoire of The Men of the Deeps

The following list is of songs which have been in the repertoire of The Men of the Deeps off and on over the past fifty years. The on-going repertoire is, of course, continuously changing and has been evolving since the choir's inception in 1966. Some of the songs have become standards, such as Rita MacNeil's "Working Man," and some may have entered the active repertoire for a short time – only to be replaced or temporarily set aside to make room for a newer, more relevant song. Ray Holland's "No. 26, One Million Ton" is a good example of such a song. The entire repertoire of songs that have been arranged for the choir over the past fifty years has grown to include upwards of 100 songs.

Initially, songs which had a direct connection with the mining industry were favoured, and although the group still diligently respects the wishes of those who inspired the founding of Cape Breton's coal miners choir, over the past five decades the repertoire has expanded to include a much wider variety of themes without abandoning the wishes of the founders of the choir. Songs documenting the history of mining in Canada, many reflecting on the good and the bad times associated with the mining industry in Cape Breton and around the world, have been joined by songs in praise of patriotism and other human emotions – especially music and poetry reflecting one's feelings for family and country – and in the case of this particular choir, songs reflecting on the beauties of Cape Breton Island. Songs that are a direct reference to the mining industry are marked with an asterisk (*).

*"**Aftermath**" by Al Provoe

A tribute to those who lost their lives in the 1992 Westray Mine Disaster, composed following a concert in Antigonish on the evening of the day the explosion took place (May 9, 1992). It is usually recited in concert as an introduction to Ron MacDonald's haunting ballad, "Their Lights Will Shine."

"**De Animal a-Comin'**" (Spiritual)

This clever little novelty song arranged by Marshall Bartholomew is classed as a "spiritual." It entered the repertoire of The Men of the Deeps very early and has particularly entertained the youngsters in the audience for the past five decades.

*"**Are You From Bevan?**" (Traditional)

Collected by Philip Thomas and published in his *Songs of the Pacific Northwest,* the song describes the effects of a strike in a small mining town in British Columbia.

"**Away From the Roll of the Sea**" by Allister MacGillivray

One of several of Allister MacGillivray's songs praising the beauties of Cape Breton Island. The song is particularly popular with Cape Bretoners away from home.

*"**The Ballad of the Frank Slide**" by Robert Gard

This song recalls a tragic avalanche in 1903 when the mining town of Frank, Alberta, almost disappeared; the enormous slide changed the shape of Turtle Mountain. The event has spawned several legends.

*"**The Ballad of J. B. McLachlan**" by Charlie MacKinnon

Charlie MacKinnon's ballad tells the story of Scottish immigrant James Bryson McLachlan and his involvement with the founding of the miners union movement in Cape Breton.

*"**The Ballad of Springhill**" by Peggy Seeger

Composed following the 1958 Springhill "Bump." Peggy was living in England at the time and was moved by the stories of heroism and heartache portrayed by the media.

"**The Banks of Newfoundland**" (Traditional)

Arranged by Howard Cable this song was one of the earliest four-part male choir arrangements to enter the repertoire of The Men of the Deeps.

*"**The Bells of Rhymney**" by Pete Seeger & Idris Davis

This song, inspired by a mining disaster in Wales, was first recorded by American folk icon, Pete Seeger using words by the Welsh poet Idris Davis. The song was a favourite of Tom Kent, a former president of DEVCO.

***"Billy, Come With Me"** by Leon Dubinsky

Given to the choir in the 1960s by the composer, the song sings of a young boy's fateful experience in the mine. It often serves as an introduction to Jim MacLellan's stories of young boys in the mines.

"Battle Hymn of the Republic" by Julia Ward Howe & William Steff

Although an American patriotic song, it never fails to emotionally move an audience.

***"Black is the Coal Dust"** by Nipper Oliver

This song sings about the infamous "company store" where credit was both a blessing and a curse. It is one of several songs to come to The Men of the Deeps from the collection of Ron MacEachern.

"Bluenose" by Dave Martins

A song in praise of Nova Scotia's famous schooner and provides an opportunity for the choir to sing the praises of another major industry in Nova Scotia.

***"Bootlegger Me"** by John McIntyre

John McIntyre's song looks at the lighter side of the illicit activity of selling bootlegged coal. Coal smuggling has persisted to a greater or lesser extent right down to the present day.

***"The Boys of the Rescue Crew"** (Traditional)

The song is a tribute to the reality of the dangers of mining, the heroism of the draegermen, and the grief of those who suffer the loss of loved ones in mine disasters.

***"The Canny Miner Lad"** by Ian Campbell

This song, originally composed for a television documentary on mining life, is set to a popular British folktune, "The Balquidder Lasses."

"Cape Breton Dream" by Dennis Ryan

This song, reminiscing of life in Cape Breton, was written by the founder and lead singer of the popular Celtic folk group, Ryan's Fancy.

"Cape Breton Silver" by Allister MacGillivray

Allister's whimsical song about mining moonshine in the woods of Cape Breton injects welcomed levity into many concerts.

"Se Ceap Breatainn" (Traditional)

Collected by Helen Creighton; a song that sings of the beauties of Cape Breton Island; the Gaelic pronunciations were mastered phonetically by members of the chorus, and the song has been most often performed as a medley with "Down Deep in a Coal Mine."

***"The Chain Runner's Song"** (Traditional)

Collected by Ron MacEachern from the singing of Edward Penny. The Men of the Deeps arrangement combines the song with another traditional tune, "When You're Done Loading Coal," also collected by Ron MacEachern – this time from the singing of Charlie MacKinnon.

***"Christmas Eve in the Mine"** A story by Jim MacLellan

This story, as told to audiences by founding member Jim MacLellan, warrants a place in the list of repertoire of the choir because it has enhanced many concerts over the years – particularly those "Mining the Soul" concerts featuring Rita MacNeil and The Men of the Deeps.

***"Christmas in the Mine"** by Paul White

Paul is a former member of the choir and served as one of the choir's valuable guitarists. The song became a staple of Rita MacNeil's "Mining the Soul Christmas" tours.

Christmas Trilogy

A trilogy of three popular Christmas songs: "O Christmas Tree," "Go Tell It On The Mountain" and "We Wish You A Merry Christmas."

***"Coal By The Sea"** by Gerard MacNeil

Gerard is a former member of the choir and composed the words to this song upon his return from the choir's tour of China in 1976. The song has been useful in educating audiences to the reality that coal mining in North America had its beginnings on Cape Breton

Island. The tune traces its roots to the Irish folk tune, "The Kerry Recruit."

*"**Coal is King Again**" by Ray Holland

Composed by Ray Holland to herald DEVCO's change of direction when falling oil prices forced the crown corporation to reverse its direction and expand coal production in Cape Breton.

*"**Coal Miner's Heaven**" by Joe Glazer

Composed and often performed by America's labour troubadour, Joe Glazer.

*"**Coal, Not Dole**" by Kay Sutcliffe

Kay was the wife of an Irish coal miner who worked the mines of Kent in England. The song, which laments the closing of England's coal mine, is arranged as a trio featuring three soloists.

*"**The Coal Owner and the Pitman's Wife**" by William Hornsby

A saucy "union" song collected by A. L. Lloyd.

*"**Coal Tattoo**" by Billy Edd Wheeler

An American songwriter from Boone County, West Virginia, Wheeler wrote this song which explains what happens when coal dust underground brushes an open skin wound.

*"**Coal Town Road**" by Allister MacGillivray

Long-time friend of The Men of the Deeps, Allister MacGillivray wrote this song recalling memories of his childhood growing up in Glace Bay. The song rivals Rita MacNeil's "Working Man" as a staple of the choir's repertoire.

*"**Dad's Old Dinner Pail**" (Traditional)

This song likely evolved from a vaudeville tune, "My Dad's Dinner Pail," by the Irish/American vaudeville artist Edward (Ned) Harrigan.

*"**Danny's Story**" as told by Jim MacLellan

The story of fourteen-year-old Danny Robinson of Springhill was recorded in George Korson's *Coal Dust on the Fiddle* and repeated in the O'Donnell publication *And Now the Fields are Green*. For many years it served as an introduction to Peggy Seeger's "The Ballad of Springhill."

*"**Dark as a Dungeon**" by Merle Travis

Arguably one of the most well-known songs about coal mining, it is rivalled only by Travis's popular "Sixteen Tons." "Dark as a Dungeon" was one of the first songs arranged for newly-formed Cape Breton coal miners chorus.

*"**Down Among The Coal**" (Traditional)

Known to Irish fiddlers as "An giolla ruadh" ("The Red Haired Boy") and popularized in Canada by John Allan Cameron as "I Am a Little Beggar Man," The Men of the Deeps arrangement is usually followed by an instrumental version with step dancer, Johnny MacLeod. (When "Papa" John passed away, son John inherited his dancing shoes.)

*"**Down Deep in a Coal Mine**" (Traditional)

Originally composed by J. B. Geoghegan in 1872 and published as "Down in a Coal Mine" in George Korson's collection, *Minstrels of the Mine Patch*.

*"**Down in the Hillcrest Mine**" by James Keelaghan

Calgary-born folksinger and composer James Keelaghan pays tribute to Alberta's Hillcrest Mine, site of the worst mining disaster in Canadian history.

"**Drill Ye Tarriers, Drill**" (Traditional)

Originally composed by Thomas F. Casey, this song pays tribute to the men who built North America's railways. The Men of the Deeps version was collected by Edith Fowke and sings the praises of the men who built the railway across Newfoundland.

*"**Dust in the Air**" by Johnny Handel

Johnny Handel is a talented bard from Northumbrian mining district of Northeast England. Getting used to being asked to sing "on the spot" while travelling, The Men of the Deeps have nicknamed this arrangement their "airport song."

*"Farewell to the Cotia" by Jock Purdham

Another song from the Northumbrian mining district of Northern England. Collected by Karl Dalla and published in his *One Hundred Songs of Toil*, he records that for reasons forgotten by all the pitmen, the Harraton Colliery in County Durham was always know as the "Cotia" – an abbreviation of Nova Scotia.

"Farewell to the Rhondda" by Frank Hennesey

This song has temporarily slipped from the regular repertoire of The Men of the Deeps. The song, describes coal mining in the district that lines the Rhondda Valley in Wales.

"Forty-Hour Week" by Dave Loggins, Lisa Silver and Don Schlitz

Initially popularized by the popular folk group Alabama, this song is a patriotic tribute to North America's working people. The Alabama version of the song concludes with a phrase from "America the Beautiful"; The Men of the Deeps conclude the song with a rousing phrase from "O Canada." The song is crowd-pleaser in both the USA and Canada.

"The Government Store" (Traditional)

Collected by Helen Creighton. A humourous song about the famed New Aberdeen (a district in Glace Bay) government store.

"Home I'll Be" by Rita MacNeil

One of Rita's many songs reminiscing about her island of Cape Breton. Often sung by Rita to signal the entrance of The Men of the Deeps during the "Mining the Soul" tours.

"If I Can't Take the Island with Me" by Aaron Lewis & Shawna Lee MacKillop

This song co-written by Aaron Lewis (formally of the Carlton Show Band) never fails to bring a tear to the eye of the many Cape Bretoners who have left the island in search of work.

"I Love Peking's Tien An Men"

A song acquired from the Canada/China Friendship Society in 1975 and sung by The Men of the Deeps during the choir's tour of The People's Republic of China in 1976.

"Immigrant Eyes" by Roger Murrah and Guy Clark

As performed by The Men of the Deeps, this song becomes a nostalgic tribute to the many immigrants who worked the mines of Cape Breton. Rita MacNeil was so fond of the song that she made it a permanent part of the "Mining the Soul" tours.

***"I'm Just an Old Chunk of Coal"** by Billy Joe Shaver

Billy Joe Shaver is a Texas country music singer and songwriter. "I'm just a old chunk of coal, but I'll be a diamond some day" provides welcome comic relief in a concert by The Men of the Deeps.

"I'm Just an Old Broken Down Mucker"

From the Phil Thomas collection, *Songs of the Pacific Northwest*.

"The Island" by Kenzie MacNeil

Kenzie MacNeil's popular song introduced in the original popular revue, *The Rise and Follies of Cape Breton Island*, was proclaimed the official anthem of Cape Breton by the Premier of Nova Scotia in May 1985.

"Isle Royale" by F. W. Gray

A song in praise of Cape Breton Island adopted by The Men of the Deeps early in the choir's career. F. W. Gray penned the song to the tune of Jan Sibelius's "Finlandia."

"I Went To Norman's" (Traditional)

Collected by Helen Creighton, the centuries-old verses of this Cape Breton song exude a romantic mood that is generally uncommon in mining songs. The choir often combines this song with another song, ***"When I First Went to Caledonia,"** also collected by Helen Creighton.

***"The Jolly Miner"** (Traditional)

Collected by Helen Creighton. One of the many "jolly miner" songs that trace its roots deep into Irish balladry. The song is usually sung today as a medley along with the song, "Jolly Wee Miner Men."

APPENDIX

*"**Jolly Wee Miner Men**" (Traditional)

Collected by George Korson from Bob Stewart, a native of Glace Bay, while Stewart was attending a convention of the United Mine Workers of America in Washington, DC.

*"**Kelly's Cove**" by Mrs. D. J. MacDonald

One of the original songs to emerge from the 1966 folksong contest. Mrs MacDonald's song is a variant of the British "Blackleg Miners"; a song about imported "scab" labour.

*"**Let's Go Workin' in a Coal Mine**" by Tony Aucoin

Composed by choir member, Tony Aucoin, the song shows off Tony's penchant for bluegrass and country music.

*"**Little Pinkie Engine**" by Ida MacAulay and John C. O'Donnell

Another of the songs to arise from the 1966 folksong contest. Relating the story of a small "saddle-type" locomotive which carried coal from Glace Bay's Caledonia Colliery to the harbour for shipment out of the island in the late 18th century. Mrs. MacAulay's song was voted best original entry in the 1966 contest. An original tune for the song was composed by director John O'Donnell.

"**The Lonely Fiddler**" by Freddie Hamood

Freddie was a former member of the choir and a very good violinist. "The Lonely Fiddler" provided a very poignant touch to the National Film Board feature documentary on The Men of the Deeps, released in 1992.

*"**Louisbourg**" by Allister MacGillivray

For many years The Men of the Deeps have been featured as part of the town of Louisbourg's summer concert series. The venue for the concerts, Louisbourg Playhouse, is a 220-seat theatre in the round. Modelled on London's 1599 Globe Theatre, the open-air playhouse was constructed at the Fortress of Louisbourg by Walt Disney Studios for the motion picture *Squanto: A Warrior's Tale*. After filming wrapped up, the structure was donated to Louisbourg and relocated to a site just off the main street of the town.

*"**The Man With a Torch in His Cap**" by Helen C. MacDonald and Leon Dubinsky

Helen MacDonald's poem was awarded the prize for best general class in the 1966 song contest. Popular Cape Breton songwriter, Leon Dubinsky, composed the music for the song.

"**Marco Polo**" by Jim Stewart

Jim Stewart's ballad recalls the glory days of the famous tall ship, *Marco Polo*. Built and launched in Saint John, New Brunswick, in 1852, it was hailed as the fastest ship in the world during the Golden Age of Sail. It sailed the world for thirty-two years and eventually sank off the coast of Cavendish, Prince Edward Island.

"**Mary Ann**" (Traditional)

A touching love song collected by Helen Creighton. The Men of the Deeps were somewhat shocked when they were asked not to sing the song in The People's Republic of China.

"**The Mary Ellen Carter**" by Stan Rogers

Another song about a famous ill-fated ship composed and made popular by Stan Rogers. Songs about ships provide an opportunity for The Men of the Deeps to explain the use of the word "deeps" as used by fishermen and coal miners.

"**Matthew's Voyage**" by Cyril MacPhee, Arnold Sampson & Wayne Touesnard

A song about John Cabot's famous ship, the *Matthew*, that reached North America in 1497 and heralded the influx of immigrants to North America.

*"**Men of the Deep**" by Bruce Guthro

Bruce dedicated this song to his father and all the men who worked the "deep" in Sydney Mines' Princess Colliery. The song provides an opportunity to explain to audiences the meaning of the work "deeps" – referring to the various coal slopes around Industrial Cape Breton which employed the coal miners who made up the membership of The Men of the Deeps.

*"**Miner's Life**" (Traditional)

The tune encouraging union miners to "stand together" derives from the Welsh hymn, "Calon Lân," and was first collected in Great Britain by A.L. Lloyd who claims that it was likely created by Welsh immigrants in America.

*"**Miner's Lullaby**" by Matt McGinn

Collected by Norman Buchanan and Peter Hall and published in *The Scottish Folksinger*.

*"**Miners' Memorial Hymn**" ("Gresford")

Verse 1 of this hymn was composed by Horatius Bonar and appears in a 1930 edition of the United Chuch Hymnal. This Gresford tune is more recent and was composed by Robert Saint to commemorate the devastating disaster at the Gresford Colliery in Wales in 1934. Verse 2 was composed specifically for The Men of the Deeps by Judith O'Donnell.

*"**A Miner and a Miner's Son**" by Tony Aucoin

Choir member, Tony Aucoin, composed this tune in memory of his father; most of the men in The Men of the Deeps followed their fathers and uncles to work in the mines. The story is different today; when it would be unusual for sons to follow their fathers into the mines.

*"**A Miner's Philosophy**" by Raymond Dvorak

A novelty song adapted from Raymond Dvorak's "Sophomoric Philosophy," a favourite among school-age children who attend concerts by The Men of the Deeps.

*"**A Mining Town no More**" by Bob Hastings

Bob Hastings composed this song in tribute to the once thriving mining town of Elliot Lake, Ontario.

*"**Mining The Devil's Coal**" by Rocky Swanson

One of the few songs in The Men of the Deeps repertoire about the downside of mining.

"My Island, Too" by Rita MacNeil

One of Rita's very early songs about her beloved island of Cape Breton.

"My Love, Cape Breton and Me" by Bob Quinn

A song in praise of the beauties of Cape Breton written by Halifax arranger, producer and pianist, Bob Quinn.

***"No More Coal"** by W. Appermont & R. Gaspercic

Belgium's famous coal miners choir, Genker Mijnwerkerskoor shared this song about the closing of the mines in Belgium with The Men of the Deeps; translation was provided by Natalie Gaspercic and adapted by Judith O'Donnell.

"Northwest Passage" by Stan Rogers

Having performed with the late Stan Rogers on more than one occasion, The Men of the Deeps delight in occasionally resurrecting one or more of the folk icon's popular ballades.

***"No. 12, New Waterford"** by Ray Holland

Ray Holland chose a popular Salvation Army tune, "He's the Lily of the Valley," for the tune of his tribute to the 1973 tragedy in New Waterford's No. 12 colliery. The ensuing fire started a chain reaction which claimed the life of 28-year old Earl Leadbeater. The grounds above the mine are now known as the Colliery Lands Park.

***"The No. 26 Mine Disaster"** by Allister MacGillivray

Allister MacGillivray's ballad pays tribute to the men who died as the result of an explosion on February 24, 1979. It tells a story of tragedy and strength in a Cape Breton mining community.

***"No. 26, One-Million Ton"** by Ray Holland

In his early days with the choir, Ray was not shy about providing his own creations to boost the repertoire of the choir. In 1892, twelve Cape Breton mines collectively produced one-million tons of coal, but the honour of being the first single mine to produce one-million tons in a year eventually went to No. 26 colliery in Glace Bay. The year was 1966, the year of the birth of The Men of the Deeps.

*"**Now That the Work is Done**" by J. P. Cormier

Multi-talented J. P. Cormier has appeared on stage many times with The Men of the Deeps. The group was delighted when J. P. produced this song lamenting the closing of the mines in Cape Breton.

"**O Canada**" Canada's national anthem (Tune by C. Lavallee)

*"**The Old Miner**" (Traditional)

A song from the United Kingdom lamenting the closing of the mines; often paired as a medley by The Men of the Deeps with another song with routes in England, "Rap Her to Bank."

*"**The Omen**" by Marie MacMillan and John C. O'Donnell

Awarded the prize for the best poem depicting a local historic event in the 1966 contest, "The Omen" tells the incredible story of an apparent supernatural happening related to the July 25, 1917, disaster at New Waterford's No. 12 Colliery.

*"**Once We Were Kings**" by Elton John

This poignant anthem is from the Broadway musical, *Billy Elliot*.

*"**Plain Old Miner Boy**" by Nell Campbell

Nell Campbell submitted this song to one of radio station CJCB's songwriting contests in the 1950s, using the American song "I'm Just a Plain Old Country Boy" for inspiration.

It received much popularity when the *Cape Breton Summertime Revue* was still known as the *Rise and Follies of Cape Breton*.

*"**The Pluck Me Store**" by Ida MacAulay and Leon Dubinsky

Ida MacAulay's poem was awarded the prize for the best traditional song in the 1966 contest, and it was set to music by Leon Dubinsky. The song recalls a day in June 1925 when several company stores in Glace Bay, New Waterford and Sydney Mines were burned to the ground.

*"**Rap Her to Bank**" (Traditional)

Published by Karl Dallas in his *One Hundred Songs of Work and Toil*, the song tells the story of miners who in the early days of the industry were required to rap (by means of a rapper rope hanging down the shaft) to signal for the cage to be wound up to the bank (surface).

*"**Remembering the Bell Island Miners**" by Wayne Rostad

Following a visit to Bell Island, Newfoundland, Wayne Rostad, host of the popular CBC television program *On the Road Again*, wrote a song in tribute to the submarine iron ore miners of Bell Island. In the late 1990s, on a concert tour of Newfoundland at the invitation of Ged Blackmoor's *Folk of the Sea*, The Men of the Deeps had the pleasure of meeting Bell Island's Submarine Miners choral group.

*"**Remember the Miner**" by Leon Dubinsky

Though it never became a permanent part of The Men of the Deeps repertoire, Leon's poignant song has been a favourite of several Cape Breton artists and groups for many years.

"**Rollin' Down to Old Maui**" by Stan Rogers

Another of Stan Rogers rollicking sea ballads.

"**Rise Again**" by Leon Dubinsky

Leon Dubinsky's famous anthem in praise of Cape Breton and its people never fails to please audiences. It's a particular favourite of school choirs who occasionally join The Men of the Deeps in an on-stage finale.

*"**The Scent of the Coal**" ("Tha Faileadh A'Ghuail") by Painter Mor

Learning the correct pronunciation of the Scottish Gaelic has delayed this arrangement from entering the permanent repertoire of the choir. Its lilting Gaelic verses tell of the conflict between mining, farming and modern industrialization on the Port Hood/Broad Cove side of Cape Breton.

*"**Schooldays End**" by Ewan MacColl

A song about young boys being called to work in the mines which provides The Men of the Deeps the opportunity to relay the story of child labour in the mines – prevalent in the 19th century.

"Sea People" by Allister MacGillivray

Another of Allister's songs praising sea-faring people scattered around the coasts of Cape Breton Island.

"She's Called Nova Scotia" by Rita MacNeil

Rita composed this song, reflecting on her beautiful home province, while she was performing at Vancouver's Expo '86.

***"A Shirt Tale"** by Danny Boutilier

A whimsical poem popular in the Springhill mining community and published by George Korson in his *Coal Dust on the Fiddle*.

***"Sixteen Tons"** by Merle Travis

Travis's song about the woes associated with the company store is another of those songs which audiences have come to expect during a concert of The Men of the Deeps.

"Song for Cape Breton" by Allister MacGillivray

Written as a tribute to many of Allister's Cape Breton heroes, "Song For Cape Breton" is another of those original songs made popular in the *Cape Breton Summertime Revue*.

"Song for the Mira" by Allister MacGillivray

Allister's most famous song has been translated into Scots Gaelic, French, Dutch and Japanese and has been recorded more than 140 times by soloists and choral groups from all over the world. It has, of course, become a standard in the repertoire of The Men of the Deeps.

***"The Springhill Disaster of 1958"** by Maurice Ruddick

Maurice began writing this song while he was trapped underground in Springhill in 1958. Regretfully, some songs in the repertoire of The Men of the Deeps, for one reason or another, do not always make it into the choir's concert list. This is one of those arrangements that have been "put on hold."

"The Star Spangled Banner" by Francis Scott Key

National anthem of the United States of America.

*"**Sweet Guinevere**" by Gordon Lightfoot

This ballad by Canadian folk icon Gordon Lightfoot was released by Lightfoot on his 1978 album *Endless Wire*.

*"**Take Me Home**" by Rod Edwards & Roger Hand

This nostalgic ballad was originally composed for the London Welsh Male Voice Choir and remains a favourite, particularly of choir's in Wales.

*"**Their Lights Will Shine**" by Ron MacDonald

Composed following the 1992 Westray disaster, this song was first recorded by Ron MacDonald's own group, Déjà vu. The song never fails to emotionally move audiences. In concert it is often preceded by Al Provoe's poem "Aftermath."

*"**Thirty-inch Coal**" by Mike Paxton

Recalling the days when coal was mined in three-foot seams, this song has become a signature entrance song for The Men of the Deeps.

*"**Today We Took a Friend from the Mine**" by Paul White

A ballad by former guitarist Paul White inspired by the death of a friend in the mine.

*"**Tramp Miner**" by Jimmie Rankin

Jimmie Rankin first recorded this song on the Rankin Family album "North Country."

*"**Trapper Boy**" by Hugh R. MacDonald

A song about a young boy's work in the mines. The song inspired MacDonald's novel, *Trapper Boy*.

*"**Underneath the Sea**" by Allister MacGillivray

This song is a tribute to the Cape Breton miners who work the mines which extend several miles under the Atlantic Ocean.

*"**The Unknown Miner's Grave**" by Mary Olive Chiasson and John C. O'Donnell.

This poignant poem was submitted as an entry in the 1966 song contest that had been organized and overseen by Helen Creighton and Nina Cohen. Although the poem did not merit a prize in that contest, the poetry seemed to be "crying out" to be put to music. The four-part arrangement was a favourite in the early days of The Men of the Deeps.

*"**When I First Went to Caledonia**" Traditional

This song, originally sung by Amby Thomas for song collector Ron MacEachern is reminiscent of many Irish/English song types deriving from the medieval pastourelle. It was also collected by Helen Creighton as "I Went to Norman's."

*"**When You're Done Loading Coal**" (Traditional)

Collected by Ronnie MacEachern from the singing of Charlie MacKinnon, The Men of the Deeps arrangement of this song is combined with another of the songs in Ronnie's collection, *The Chain Runner's Song*.

*"**With A Shovel In His Hand**" by Lillian Crewe Walsh and John C. O'Donnell

This tribute to the Cape Breton coal miner was a poem written long before The Men of the Deeps came into being. It was set to music because it fulfilled its purpose of introducing the Cape Breton miner to early audiences.

*"**Working at the Coal Face**" by Dave Webber

Known equally as well in the United States and in the United Kingdom, Dave Webber's song describes life underground from three different points of view.

*"**Working Man**" by Rita MacNeil

Unofficial anthem of the working man, The Men of the Deeps first teamed up with Rita MacNeil to sing this song in 1984.

"**You'll be Home Again**" by Allister MacGillivray

Allister's nostalgic dream of home (Cape Breton) is a favourite at home and away.

"You Raise Me Up" by Brendan Graham & Rolf Løvland

This uplifting song is so popular that it has never been out of the charts somewhere in the world. It has been recorded in more than seventeen languages by many of the world's greatest artists and choir's.

***"The Westville Miners"** by Eugene Johnson

Eugene Johnson was one of twenty-six miners killed in the Westray Explosion in Plymouth, Nova Scotia. Eugene's song about his fellow miners from Westville and the other New Glasgow towns surrounding the Westray area came to the attention of The Men of the Deeps after that fateful day in May 1992. Shane MacLeod was soloist on this arrangement.

***"Who Are They?"** By Al Provoe

Former member Al Provoe was a talented poet as well as an excellent singer. The final line of his poem, "Who Are They?," was chosen as the title for the publication *And Now The Fields Are Green*. The poem has become a standard in the repertoire of The Men of the Deeps and is usually recited in concert by Gordon Sheriff.

Appendix 5

The Men of the Deeps Recordings

Choral Arrangements – Jack O'Donnell (Except those marked *)

1968: *The Men of the Deeps* (Apex, LP)

Side 1: The Cape Breton Coal Miners (by Ray Holland)
    Drill Ye Tarriers, Drill (traditional)
    The Ballad of Springhill (by Peggy Seeger)
    Little Pinkie Engine (by Ida MacAulay & John C. O'Donnell)
    Dark as a Dungeon (by Merle Travis)
Side 2: Hey, Look Me Over (by Carol Leigh)*
    Mary Ann (traditional) col. by Helen Creighton*
    De Animals a' Comin' (Spiritual)*
    Aura Lee (by W. W. Fosdick & G. K. Poulton)*
    Dry Bones (Spiritual)*
    Jolly Wee Miner Men (traditional, col. by George Korson)

1975: *The Men of the Deeps* (Waterloo, LP)

Side 1: The Cape Breton Coal Miners (by Ray Holland)
    Schooldays End (by Ewan MacColl)
    No. 26, One Million Ton (by Ray Holland)
    The Pluck Me Store (by Ida MacAulay & Leon Dubinsky)
    Dark as a Dungeon (by Merle Travis)
    Little Pinkie Engine (by Ida MacAulay & John C. O'Donnell)

Side 2: Oran: Do Ceap Breattain (traditional, col. by Helen Creighton)
    Down Deep in a Coal Mine (traditional)
    Sixteen Tons (by Merle Travis)*
    The Omen (by Marie MacMillian & John C. O'Donnell)
    No. 12, New Waterford (by Ray Holland)
    Miners' Memorial Hymn ("Gresford")
    Jolly Wee Miner Men (traditional, col. by George Korson)

1977: *The Men of the Deeps II* (Waterloo, LP)

Side 1: The Man With a Torch in His Cap (by MacDonald & Dubinsky)
    The Ballad of Springhill (by Peggy Seeger)
    Isle Royale (by F. W. Gray)*
    The Jolly Miner (traditional, col. by Helen Creighton)
    The Battle Hymn of the Republic (by J. W. Howe & W. Steffe)*

Side 2: Drill Ye Tarriers, Drill (traditional)
    Mary Ann (traditional, col. by Helen Creighton)*
    The Banks of Newfoundland (traditional, arr. by Howard Cable)*
    The Government Store (traditional, col. by Helen Creighton)
    The Coal by the Sea (by Gerard MacNeil)
    Swing Low, Sweet Chariot (traditional)*

1984: *The Men of the Deeps III* (Waterloo, LP)

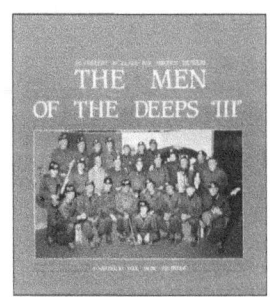

Side 1: Coal Tattoo (by Billy Edd Wheeler)
    The Canny Miner (by Ian Campbell)
    Plain Ol' Miner Boy (by Nel Campbell)
    The Lonely Fiddler (by Freddie Hamood)
    No. 26 Mine Disaster (by Allister MacGillivray)
    The Ballad of Jim McLachlan (by Charlie MacKinnon)
    Dust in the Air (by Johnny Handel)
Side 2: Song for the Mira (by Allister MacGillivray)
    Sea People (by Allister MacGillivray)
    Cape Breton Silver (by Allister MacGillivray)
    Cape Breton Dream (by Dennis Ryan)
    The Unknown Miner's Grave (by M. Chiasson & J. O'Donnell)
    Coal is King Again (by Ray Holland)
    Rap 'er to Bank (traditional)

1991: *Diamonds in the Rough* (Men of the Deeps label, CD)

    Thirty-inch Coal (by Mike Paxton)
    Dark as a Dungeon (by Merle Travis)
    Coal Tattoo (by Billy Edd Wheeler)
    Sixteen Tons (by Merle Travis)*
    I Went to Norman's (traditional, col. by Helen Creighton)
    Man With a Torch in His Cap (by H. MacDonald & L. Dubinsky)
    Coal is King Again (by Ray Holland)
    Working Man (by Rita MacNeil)
    The Coal by the Sea (by Gerard MacNeil)
    Mary Ann (traditional, col. by Helen Creighton)
    Are You From Bevan? (traditional, col. by Phil Thomas)
    Dust in the Air (by Johnny Handel)
    Plain Ole Miner Boy (by Nel Campbell)
    No. 26 Mine Disaster (by Allister MacGillivray)
    Farewell to the Rhondda (by Frank Hennessey)
    Rise Again (by Leon Dubinsky)

1995: *Men of the Deeps: Buried Treasures* (Atlantica, CD from vinyl compilation)

Contents: The Jolly Miner (traditional, col. by Helen Creighton)
    Little Pinkie Engine (by Ida MacAulay & John C. O'Donnell)
    The Government Store (traditional, col. by Helen Creighton)
    The Omen (by Marie MacMillan & John C. O'Donnell)
    Jolly Wee Miner Men (traditional, col. by Helen Creighton)
    The Ballad of Springhill (by Peggy Seeger)
    The Unknown Miner's Grave (by M. Chiasson & J. O'Donnell)
    Kelly's Cove (traditional)
    Miner's Memorial Hymn ("Gresford")
    Oran Do Ceap Breattain / Down Deep in a Coal Mine (trad.)
    Coal is King Again (by Ray Holland)
    Cape Breton Dream (by Dennis Ryan)
    The Cape Breton Coal Miners (by Ray Holland)
    The Lonely Fiddler (by Freddie Hamood)
    Drill Ye Tarriers, Drill (traditional)

1996: *Coal Fire in Winter* (Atlantica, CD)

Contents: Tramp Miner (by Jimmy Rankin)
    Coal, Not Dole (by Kay Sutcliffe)
    Billy, Come With Me (by Leon Dubinsky)
    Dad's Old Dinner Pail (traditional)
    She Loves Her Miner Lad (traditional)
    Sweet Guinevere (by Gordon Lightfoot)
    You'll Be Home Again (by Allister MacGillivray)
    Miner's Life (traditional)
    The Banks of Newfoundland (arr. by H. Cable)*
    Rollin' Down to Old Maui (by Stan Rogers)
    If I Can't Take the Island With Me (by McKillop & Lewis)
    Coal Town Road (by Allister MacGillivray)
    Who Are They (by Al Provoe)*
    Working Man (by Rita MacNeil)

2004: *Their Lights Will Shine* (The Men of the Deeps label, CD)

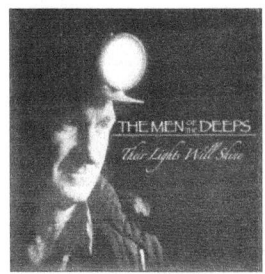

Contents: A Miner and a Miner's Son (by Tony Aucoin)
    Men of the Deep (by Bruce Guthro)
    Matthew's Voyage (by Cyril MacPhee et al.)
    The Jolly Miner Medley (traditional)
    I'm Just an Old Chunk of Coal (by Joe Shaver)
    Immigrant Eyes (by Guy Clark et al.)
    The Mary Ellen Carter (by Stan Rogers)
    Drill Ye Tarriers, Drill (traditional)
    The Hillcrest Mine (by James Keeleghan)
    Song for the Mira (by Allister MacGillivray)
    Their Lights Will Shine (by Ron MacDonald)
    A Mining Town no More (by Bob Hastings)
    Rise Again (by Leon Dubinsky)

2007: *Forty Years Young* (The Men of the Deeps label, CD)

Contents: Thirty-inch Coal (by Mike Paxton)
    The Cape Breton Coal Miners (by Ray Holland)
    The Ballad of Joe Hill (by Hayes & Robinson)
    Schooldays End (by Ewan MacColl)
    The Ballad of Springhill (by Peggy Seeger)
    Miner's Memorial Hymn ("Gresford")
    Farewell to the Cotia (by Jock Purdham)
    No More Coal (by W. Appermont & R. Gaspercic)

Now That the Work is Done (by J.P. Cormier)
The Old Miner (traditional)
Rap Her to Bank (traditional)
Away From the Roll of the Sea (by Allister MacGillivray)
The Marco Polo (by Jim Stewart)
She's Called Nova Scotia (by Rita MacNeil)

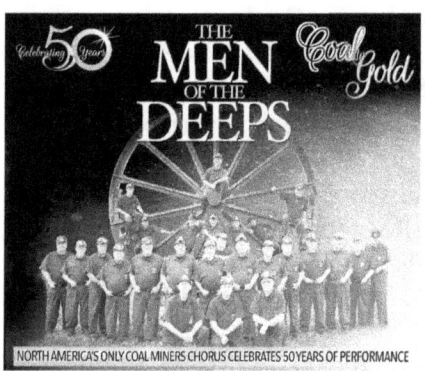

2016: *Coal to Gold* (The Men of the Deeps label, Compilation CD)

From *The Men of the Deeps* (Apex, LP, 1967)
    "The Cape Breton Coal Miners" (by Ray Holland)
    "Miners Memorial Hymn" ("Gresford")

From *The Men of the Deeps* (Waterloo, LP, 1975)
    "Little Pinkie Engine" (by Ida MacAulay and John C. O'Donnell)
    "Dark as a Dungeon" (by Merle Travis)
    "Sixteen Tons" (by Merle Travis)

From *The Men of the Deeps II* (Waterloo LP, 1977)
    "The Man With a Torch in his Cap" (by H. C. MacDonald & Leon Dubinsky)
    "Mary Ann" (traditional, col. by Helen Creighton)*

From *The Men of the Deeps III* (Waterloo, LP, 1984)
    "Unknown Miners Grave" (by Mary O. Chiasson & John C. O'Donnell)
    "Coal is King Again" (by Ray Holland)

From *Diamonds in the Rough* (The Men of the Deeps label. Compact Disc) 1991
    "Dust In The Air" (by Johnny Handel)

"Coal Tattoo" (by Billy Edd Wheeler)
"The Coal by the Sea" (by Gerard MacNeil)
"No. 26 Mine Disaster" (by Allister MacGillivray)
From *Men of the Deeps: Buried Treasures* (Atlantica, CD, 1995)
"Oran do Ceap Breattain" / "Down Deep in a Coal Mine" (traditional)

From *Coal Fire In Winter* (Atlantica, CD, 1996)
"Working Man" (by Rita MacNeil)
"Dad's Old Dinner Pail" (traditional)

From *Mining The Soul: Rita MacNeil with The Men of the Deeps*
(Lupins Entertainment, CD, 2000)
"Plain Ole Miner Boy" (by Nel Campbell)
"Immigrant Eyes" (by Guy Clark et al)

From *Their Lights Will Shine* (The Men of the Deeps label, CD, 2004)
"Men of the Deeps" (by Bruce Guthro)
"The Jolly Miner Medley" (traditional)
"A Miner and a Miner's Son" (by Tony Aucoin)
"Song for the Mira" (by Allister MacGillivray)

From *Forty Years Young* (The Men of the Deeps label, CD, 2007)
"Thirty-Inch Coal" (by Mike Paxton)
"No More Coal" (by W. Appermont & R. Gaspercic)
"The Ballad of Springhill" (by Peggy Seeger)

From *Coal to Gold* (The Men of the Deeps label, CD, 2016)
"Trapper Boy" (by Hugh MacDonald)
"Working at the Coal Face" (by Dave Webber)
"Home I'll Be" (by Rita MacNeil, arr. by Stephen Muise)
*These three songs were recorded in 2016, and featured:
Stephen Muise – Piano / Keyboard / Accordion / Percussion
Fred Lavery – Guitar / Bass
Shane MacLeod – Bass (Working at the Coal Face)
Fiddle – Kimberly Fraser
Producer – Stephen Muise
Engineer – Mike Sheppard
Conductor – Jack O'Donnell
Arrangements – Jack O'Donnell (except "Home I'll Be")
Bonus Track – "Drill Ye Terriers Drill" (traditional)

Notes

Notes Foreword

1. Frank, "Coal Masters and Coal Miners," 1971; "The Miner's Financier" 1983; The Industrial Folksong in Cape Breton, 1986; *J. B. McLachlan: A Biography*, 1999; Hornsby *Nineteenth Century Cape Breton* 1992; MacGillivray, "Military Aid to the Civil Power," 1974; Muise, "The Making of an Industrial Community," 1980.

2. Hornsby, "Staple Trades, Subsistence Agriculture," 1989: 423.

3. Ibid.

4. McKay, "By Wisdom, Wile or War," 1986: 18.

5. MacKinnon, "A Typology of Cape Breton Island Company Housing," 2016.

6. Muise 1980: 78.

7. Ibid.: 77.

8. Hornsby 1992: 178.

9. Muise 1980: 82.

10. Ibid.: 79.

11. Boutlilier, *New Waterford: 3 Generations*, 1988: 4.

12. Millward, "Mine Locations and the Sequence of Coal Exploitation," 1985: 183.

13. Ibid.: 199. North side and south side of Sydney Harbour.

14. Ibid.: 200.

15. Harry Petrie, "Tab for the Dominion Coal Company," 1918.

16. Boutilier, 1988: 31.

17. Davey and MacKinnon, *Dictionary of Cape Breton English*, 2016: 125.

18. Daniel Petrie, dir., *The Bay Boy*, 1986.

19. O'Donnell, *And Now the Fields Are Green*, 1992: 86.

20. Davey and MacKinnon, 17.

21. Williston, *Johnny Miles: Nova Scotia's Marathon King*, 1990: 13.

22. See, for example, Brasset, *A Doctor's Pilgrimage*, 1951.

23. UNESCO, 2003.

24. Frank, 1993: 247.

25. Akerman, *Black Around the Eyes*, 1981: 76.

26. Frank, 1999: 374.

Notes to Prologue

1. MacGillivray, *Diamonds In The Rough*, 1991: 65; *The Men of the Deeps – The Continuing Saga,* 2000: 71.

2. MacGillivray, *Diamonds in the Rough*.

3. MacGillivray, *The Continuing Saga*.

4. MacGillivray, *Diamonds In The Rough*, 12; *The Continuing Saga*. Glace Bay, 20.

5. Bob MacLeod in MacGillivray, *The Continuing Saga*, 23.

6. Aaron Beswick, the *Chronicle Herald*, May 2, 2015.

7. The choir had not disbanded when I left for England; following Expo '67 and the production of its first recording, the group had remained together, with the help of other directors, for the pure love of singing. Apparently, however, officials at DEVCO had determined that the repertoire of the choir was beginning to stray from its original mandate.

8. O'Donnell, *And Now the Fields are Green*, 1992.

9. Seeger, *English Folk Music Journal*, Vol. 6, No. 5 (1994).

Notes Chapter 1

1. *Cape Breton Post*, November 4, 1966.

2. The name "The Men of the Deeps" came about rather spontaneously when, at a rehearsal prior to the Expo '67 performances, Nina asked for ideas for a name. Someone called out: "We come from the deeps; we're the men of the deeps!" – the "deeps" being a reference to the mine slopes in Cape Breton which extend out beneath the floor of the Atlantic Ocean.

3. *Cape Breton Post*, November 6, 1966.

4. *Cape Breton Post*, November 4, 1966.

5. The 1966 song writing contest, organized by Nina Cohen and overseen by Dr. Helen Creighton, attracted contributors ranging in age from a 12-year old girl to a woman of 100. Prizes were awarded in seven different categories: Best original song, "Little Pinkie Engine" (contributed by Ida MacAulay); best humourous song, "Bootlegger Me" (contributed by John McIntyre); best song depicting a local historic event, "The Omen" (contributed by Marie MacMillan);

best general class, "The Man with a Torch in His Cap" (contributed by Helen C. MacDonald); best song from a contributor over 90 years of age, "Kelly's Cove" (contributed by Mrs. D. J. MacDonald); best song from a contributor under the age of 16, "The Miner" (contributed by Donna Troicuk); and best traditional song, "The Pluck Me Store" (contributed by Ida MacAulay).

6. More on the repertoire of The Men of the Deeps can be found in appendices to this publication.

7. Originally collected by A. L. Lloyd as "I Love My Miner Lad."

8. *Cape Breton Post*, March 25, 1968.

9. Although I was involved to an extent in those early recording sessions, there was a stronger reality looming in my life. When I learned that I had been accepted to do graduate studies in England at London's King's College, I truly thought that that would be the end of my adventure with The Men of the Deeps. In fact, there was no indication that the group would continue beyond the recording project. I was totally thrilled when, in the midst of my London graduate school experience, I received in the mail a copy of the finished product: *The Men of the Deeps: North America's Only Coal Miners Choir* (Apex). That recording is no longer in circulation. In fact, it is so much out of circulation that it recently showed up in an antique store in Nova Scotia. A close friend purchased the "antique" recording and presented it to me!

10. With my main focus on my studies in London, I knew nothing of all of this. But in retrospect I know it was a good period for the choir, and Fred's talent and wit instilled even more confidence in the members of the group.

11. Teresa Ann MacLellan, known by all as Ann Terry (and by those closest to her as Terry), was an extraordinary woman, and it is fortuitous that her path crossed with that of The Men of the Deeps. Her popularity as a radio and television personality made her in much demand throughout the island as master of ceremonies for community events and, until the early 1970s, she was also in demand for a variety of interviews, commercials, coverage of royal visits as well as numerous guest appearances on CBC's popular *Front Page Challenge*. When Terry left her radio/television career for a position as Director of Tourism with the Cape Breton Development Corporation, her experience in the broadcasting industry proved to be a great asset. She saw tourism as sharing in the progress of Cape Breton, and her many projects exemplified this ideology. Her work eventually culminated in her promotion to Director of Corporate Affairs in 1980, a position she held until her death in 1985.

12. "Coal is King Again," by Ray Holland.

Notes Chapter 2

1. The reputation of The Men of the Deeps received a great boost when the magazine *Audio Scene* promoted that first distributed recording with Waterloo Music Company as "The best single album of Canadiana in almost a decade." The publishers were so pleased with the success of the 1975 recording that they

immediately made plans for a second LP recording, *The Men of the Deeps II*. That second Waterloo recording was released in 1977.

2. "The Ryans and The Pittmans," more popularly known as "We'll Rant and We'll Roar," is based on a traditional English sea shanty.

3. Official relations were established in 1970, after Canadian Prime Minister Pierre Elliott Trudeau recognized the People's Republic of China, becoming one of the first Western countries to do so. Canada has deep cultural links with China, being home to a large Chinese diaspora.

4. Special credit should be given to Paige Hunter, secretary to the Department of Music at St. Francis Xavier University. Her meticulous records of potential and solid donors constituted an immeasurable contribution to the success of the entire project.

5. Cameron, "Behind the Rising Sun."

6. The group would meet Pierre Berton again when, in the following year, The Men of the Deeps were to appear on the popular CBC television program, *Front Page Challenge*. (Mr. Berton was a popular panelist on that show.)

7. In the midst of our preparations for the trip to China I had received a visit from noted author and journalist, Silver Donald Cameron. I had never met Don, but I knew of his work through his writings. In particular, I recalled his wonderful article on Dr. Helen Creighton published in *Weekend Magazine* late in 1974. Until Don's visit, I had not given any thought to how, or even if, this planned concert tour of The People's Republic of China might be covered by the press. When he suggested that, because diplomatic relations between Canada and China were still in their infancy, this tour might have special significance, I listened.

We had received authorization from the government of The People's Republic of China for our choir to tour the country. No permission had been granted for an accompanying journalist. What to do? Simple. Don was added to our roster as a first tenor. Problem solved.

That proved to be a decision that we would not regret. Silver Donald Cameron fit into the group immediately and his memorable series of articles on the trip later published in *Weekend Magazine* over four consecutive weeks in November and December of 1976, gave credence to the proclamation of the Ottawa *Journal* that The Men of the Deeps tour of China was "the best people-to-people exchange ever" between our two countries.

8. Cameron: "A Tale of Two Chinas."

9. Ibid.

10. Before embarking on our tour of The People's Republic of China I had befriended members of the Halifax chapter of the Chinese Friendship Society. It was through them that I learned of a song that was currently very popular

in China, "I Love Peking's Tienanmen" (a tribute to Beijing's famous square) which I promptly arranged for four-part male choir. We sang it frequently for our Chinese audiences and always received a bemused but approving response. The people of China, at that time, were simply not attuned to our European-based style of harmony.

11. Cameron, "A Tale of Two Chinas."

12. *Cape Breton Post*: July 1976

13. "Miners' Memorial Hymn," credited to Horatio Bonar; Verse 2, composed in 1966 by Judith O'Donnell.

14. Cameron, "Marx, Mao and Morality."

15. Cameron, "Underground in China. Apparently, a similar system had been experimented with in Cape Breton where gas was pumped from the wall face to the surface, but because of the distance from the wall face to the surface (7 miles), it was deemed unsafe.

16. The Marble Boat (also known as the Boat of Purity and Ease) serves as a lakeside pavilion on the grounds of the Summer Palace. Originally constructed in 1755, it was destroyed in 1860 during the Second Opium War. The Empress Dowager, Cixi, ordered its restoration in 1893, apparently using money that was intended to create a new imperial navy.

17. The museum later suffered a major fire and the valuable art work was slightly damaged, having been among the items rescued from the fire. It currently hangs in the restored museum theatre.

Notes Chapter 3

1. The late Hon. Flora MacDonald was also a guest of Peter Gzowski on that program. Later, in her capacity as Minister of Communications in Brian Mulroney's government, the Cape Breton native would be responsible for obtaining funding for The Men of the Deeps appearances at another World's Fair: Expo '86 in Vancouver.

2. Cameron, "A Tale of Two Chinas."

3. *Mines & Matter*, Cape Breton Development Corporation, vol. 3, no. 4.

4. The 1979 Nova Scotia Tattoo was actually the second appearance of The Men of the Deeps in the presence of the Queen Mother. In 1967, Her Majesty was guest of honour at a centennial year celebration in Sydney's Wentworth Park. It was perhaps a sign of her sharp memory and her ability to connect with people that, on the occasion of the meeting in Halifax in 1979, she recalled vividly the first time she had heard The Men of the Deeps in Sydney, in 1967.

5. Coincidentally, the nurse on duty that fateful morning was Carol Sheriff, wife of long-time member, Gordon Sheriff.

6. Earl Leadbeater was the uncle of The Men of the Deeps drummer, Ronnie Leadbeater.

Notes Chapter 4

1. "Digging out the best in TV": *TV Guide*, 1983. Ken Larone, Editor, commenting on The Men of the Deeps participation in the CanPro Awards celebration held in Halifax.

2. From the early 1970s, the Canadian Folk Music Society (now the Canadian Society for Traditional Music) strongly influenced the music that would make up the repertoire of The Men of the Deeps. Through that society I became acquainted with some of Canada's most seasoned folksong collectors, and in the late 1970s, I was privileged to serve as president of the organization.

3. A song collected by Dr. Fowke became the tune for one of The Men of the Deeps most significant songs, "The Coal by the Sea" (words by former member Gerard MacNeil).

4. Thomas, *Songs of the Pacific Northwest*.

5. Korson, *Coal Dust on the Fiddle*.

6. O'Donnell, 142.

7. Unfortunately, Ann Terry's tenure as an honorary member was short-lived; on June 15, 1985, she succumbed to cancer. It was a sad day for The Men of the Deeps, and indeed, for all of Cape Breton.

8. See note 1.

9. The 1980s was also productive for the research aspect of my relationship with The Men of the Deeps. Having been appointed to the Order of Canada in 1983, I had gained enough confidence to apply for a Canadian Heritage grant from the Department of Secretary of State. The grant was awarded in 1984 and enabled me to spend much of my sabbatical year researching the relationship between songs from the coal fields of Great Britain and those of Nova Scotia. The results of that research provided me with much material which I would eventually publish in various academic journals. Those articles were often the result of papers presented to major conferences in the United States and Canada.

10. The Men of the Deeps arrangement of Rita's "Working Man" has proven to be so popular with choirs around the world, that I have received requests for arrangements representing a wide variety of choral combinations – including not only the obvious four-part male (TTBB) and mixed choir (SATB and SAB) arrangements, but more specialized groups such as barbershop quartets and gospel choirs have also expressed an interest in performing Rita's iconic anthem.

11. It is regrettable that long-time mentor and advocate for The Men of the Deeps, Ann Terry MacLellan did not live to celebrate this important milestone for the group.

12. *Cape Breton Post*, Sydney, Nova Scotia. 4.

13. The Westray Mine disaster of 1992 and its effect on The Men of the Deeps will be discussed in Chapter 5.

14. "She Loves Her Miner Lad" was first collected by A. L. Lloyd as "I Love My Miner Lad" and published in *Singing Englishmen*. The song is descended from a long line of "Jolly Miner" songs which trace their origin to an old Irish ballad, "The Bonny Labouring Boy." Two other ballads in the repertoire of The Men of the Deeps also descend from the same root: "The Jolly Miner" and "Jolly Wee Miner Men."

15. Murray Ginsberg: *International Musician*, December 1986.

16. Chris Dafoe, *Globe and Mail*, June 24, 1989.

17. MacGillivray, *Diamonds in the Rough*.

Notes Chapter 5

1. From Thomas McGrath's poem, "Coal Fire in Winter," see p. 51.

2. The Antigonish *Casket*, April 10, 1991.

3. In addition to Harvey Webber, the committee consisted of Mack Haley, Jim Inch, Helen Marshall, Trudy MacDonald, Barry MacKinnon, John Nash, Carl Turner and Dan White.

4. MacGillivray, *Diamonds in the Rough*.

5. Draegermen are miners, members of a special crew, trained in underground rescue work. Named for Alexander B. Dräger (d. 1928), German scientist and inventor of the rescue equipment.

6. "Their Lights Will Shine" later became the title song of The Men of the Deeps 2004 CD release (see chapter 6).

7. CBU Press, 1992. In the following year I was granted an honorary Doctor of Letters degree from UCCB (now Cape Breton University) in recognition of my work with The Men of the Deeps and in recognition of my publications. In the year 2000, the University granted the entire membership of the choir an honorary degree in recognition of the choir's contribution to culture in Cape Breton's mining communities.

8. It was also in 1997 (July/August) that I was fortunate enough to spend three weeks at a the Tyrone Guthrie Centre for the arts – a unique colony for musicians, writers and artists in Annaghmakerrig, County Monahan, Ireland. The experience, funded by a Canada Council Grant, enabled me to compose new musical arrangements and lay out a plan for my future involvement with The Men of the Deeps.

9. Sadly, it was following the 1998 tour of Newfoundland that The Men of the Deeps president, Angus MacDonald died of cancer.

10. Thomas McGrath's "Coal Fire in Winter" first appeared in News of the Universe: *Poems of Twofold Consciousness*. Sierra Club Books, 530 Bush Street, San Francisco, California, 94108.

11. MacGillivray, *The Continuing Saga*, 156.

12. Ibid.

13. THANK YOU, NATO. TONI BLAIR, (Bill) CLINTON, (Gerhard) SCHRÖDER, ROBIN COOK, (Jacques) CHIRAC, (Madeleine) ALBRIGHT.

14. I was particularly pleased to be asked to assist Lebo M at the afternoon rehearsal. The rehearsal session was a joy, but reality set in when we received a bomb scare toward the conclusion of the rehearsal. Fortunately, it turned out to be just that – a "scare."

15. Heavily armed soldiers were present, stationed strategically among the large audience.

16. MacGillivray, *The Continuing Saga*, 156.

17. Tenor, Matt Breski qtd. in MacGillivray, Ibid.

18. UNICEF/UNHCR press release.

Notes Chapter 6

1. Silver Donald Cameron: *Globe and Mail*, February 15, 1999.

2. Approval and encouragement for The Men of the Deeps from the people of Cape Breton didn't stop with the honorary degree bestowed upon the group in 2000, or the "Walk of Stars" recognition in that same year; the community came together again in 2003 to show further support. Recognizing my contribution as long-term musical director, I was honoured with a testimonial dinner as part of an extensive fundraising campaign in support of Glace Bay's Cape Breton Miners' Museum hosted by my long-time friend, Halifax entrepreneur and philanthropist, Charles Keating.

3. In addition to Harvey Webber, those committee members included Eileen Lannon Oldford, Valerie Bobyk, Tracy Boutilier, David Ein, Marg Ellsworth, Barry MacKinnon, Vince McGillivray, John Nash, Carl Turner, Wayne Weatherbee and Dan White.

4. A recipient of an honorary degree from Cape Breton University in 1995, Daniel Petrie eventually succumbed to his illness and passed away in August 2004 at the age of 83.

5. Recognizing Redgrave's interest and involvement in numerous humanitarian projects throughout her career – particularly with regard to her affiliation with the United Nations – I was happy to have the opportunity before leaving Kosovo to familiarize her with the work at St. Francis Xavier University's Coady International Institute. The conversation culminated in her agreeing to entertain the possibility of accepting an honorary degree from St. FX if she were approached. The invitation was extended to her by then university president Sean Riley shortly after The Men of the Deeps returned from Kosovo. (The Men were unable to attend en mass, but second tenor Gordon Sheriff and his wife, Carol, were able to represent the group at the Antigonish event.)

6. It was necessary for her to leave immediately following the convocation to

catch a previously arranged private plane for New York where she was scheduled to speak at a dinner at Lincoln Center honouring actress Jane Fonda. I was amused the following day when I received a fax from Vanessa informing me that she had again recited the poem, "Coal Fire in Winter," at that affair.

7. *Chorus: Nova Scotia Choral Federation Newsletter*, vol. 26, No. 1, Summer 2001.

8. The tune, "Down Among the Coal" – known to Irish fiddlers as "An giolla ruadh" ("The Red Haired Boy") – has been used for countless traditional songs. In Nova Scotia, and indeed throughout Canada, the tune was popularized by the late John Allan Cameron as "I Am A Little Beggar Man." Apparently, the melody is one of the relatively few common to fiddlers throughout Scotland and Ireland, and it was transferred nearly intact to the North American fiddle traditions. In the United States it has been a favourite of bluegrass fiddlers in recent times.

9. "Papa John" is the father of fellow tenors Nipper MacLeod and John MacLeod, Jr.

10. That concert at Hummingbird Centre provided another opportunity for The Men to meet yet another celebrity when Canadian contralto Maureen Forrester appeared backstage to extend her appreciation to the group for its contribution to culture in Canada.

11. Neither Stephen nor Ronnie – nor myself – can be considered official full-fledged members of The Men of the Deeps because none of us has had the experience of working in a coal mine. In concerts, Stephen often announces to the audience that "these men have earned the right to wear the official stage uniform of coveralls and hard hats because they have all fulfilled the requirement for membership of having worked a minimum of two years underground in a mine." In other words, the reality is that in order to become a singing member of The Men of the Deeps, the second requirement is the ability to sing; the first requirement is that you must have experience working underground.

12. It is not uncommon in Cape Breton for musicians and performers, in a show of solidarity and support, to appear in a back-up roll on each other's recording ventures.

13. Feed Nova Scotia Annual Report, 2006-2007. www.feednovascotia.ca.

14. Also performing for MineExpo that week – although in another locale – was Grammy Award winner, Lionel Ritchie.

15. That experience was later release as a DVD titled *Rita MacNeil, Live in Concert with The Men of the Deeps*.

Notes Chapter 7

1. *Oran*: "*Tha faileadh a' ghuail*" as printed in O'Donnell.

2. *Canadian Mining Journal*, May 2010.

3. Fergusson, *Beyond the Hebrides*, 1977.

4. Apparently, because at the time of their deaths their religion was not known, they were not allowed to be buried in the churchyard proper. Instead, these migrant miners were buried outside the gate of the cemetery. Part of the dedication ceremonies associated with the unveiling of the monument included the acceptance of those places of rest into the churchyard cemetery proper.

5. All were pleased when in 2013 Joe Shannon was made an Officer of the Order of Canada, and again in 2014 when he was recognized with an honorary doctoral degree from St. Francis Xavier University.

6. It turned out that Adrian's sister, Shirl Boughner, had been a fan of The Men of the Deeps ever since, at the age of 15, she had enjoyed the fledgeling choir's performances at Expo '67 in Montreal.

7. Joe White's enjoyed a moment of glory one Sunday morning when The Men of the Deeps were en route to a concert in Yarmouth. Choir member Bobby Roper realized while en route that he had forgotten to pack his mining helmet (part of the required stage gear worn during every concert). Remembering that Joe had been given a mining helmet (complete with lamp) several years earlier to celebrate his friendship with the choir, the group made a decision to stop at Joe's home in Antigonish to borrow Joe's helmet. Joe could not have had a finer moment!

8. Established in 1969, Daybreak was the first L'Arche community in Canada.

9. http://indianriverfestival.com/.

10. Lorna MacDonald is Professor of Voice and the Lois Marshall Chair in Voice Studies at the University of Toronto. Her singing has won her awards that took her to New York's Metropolitan Opera, the Graz Stephaniensaal, Shreveport Opera, Los Angeles' Disney Hall, and to a remote village in Ghana for African singing and drumming. Lorna is the creator and producer of *The Bells of Baddeck—the Alexander Graham and Mabel Bell Story* which had its successful debut in 2015 at the Alexander Graham Bell Museum in Baddeck.

Notes Epilogue

1. In April 2016 Gordon succeeded Shane MacLeod as president of The Men of the Deeps.

2. See Appendix 4 for the complete repertoire and Appendix 5 for a list of recordings.

Bibliography

Akerman, Jeremy. *Black Around the Eyes*. Toronto: McClelland and Stewart, 1981.

Boutilier, Ted. *New Waterford: 3 Generations*. New Waterford: Town of New Waterford, privately published, 1988.

Bowen, Lynne. *Boss Whistle: The Coal Miners of Vancouver Island Remember*. Lantzville, BC: Oolichan Books. 1982.

Brasset, Dr. Edmund A. *A Doctor's Pilgrimage*. Philadelphia: Lippincott, 1951.

Burns, Sean. *Archie Green: The Making of a Hero*. Chicago: University of Illinois Press, 2013.

Cameron, Silver Donald. "Behind the Rising Sun," *Weekend Magazine*, November 22, 1976.

———. "Silver Donald Cameron in the Mysterious East, Part I: Underground in China," *Weekend Magazine*, November 27, 1976.

———. "Silver Donald Cameron in the Mysterious East, Part II: A Tale of Two Cities," *Weekend Magazine*, December 4, 1976.

———. Silver Donald Cameron in the Mysterious East, Part III: Marx, Mao and Morality, Part III," *Weekend Magazine*, December 11, 1976.

Creighton, Helen. *Maritime Folk Songs*. Toronto: Doubleday Canada, 1980.

———. *Songs and Ballads of Nova Scotia*. New York: Dover Publications, Inc. 1966.

Currie, Sheldon. *Down the Coaltown Road*. Toronto: Key Porter Books, 2002.

Dallas, Karl. *One Hundred Songs of Work and Toil*. London: Wolfe Publishing, 1974.

Endicott, Stephen L. *Bienfait. The Saskatchewan Miners' Struggle of '31*. Toronto: University of Toronto Press, 2002.

Fergusson, Donald A. *Beyond the Hebrides*. Halifax: Donald A Fergusson/Lawson Graphics Atlantic, 1977.

Fowke, Edith. *The Penguin Book of Canadian Folk Songs*. Harmondsworth: Penguin, 1973.

———. "Labour and industrial protest songs in Canada," Journal of American Folklore, 82:323 (1969).

——— and Joe Glazer. *Songs of Work and Protest*. New York: Dover Publications, 1973.

Fox, Maier B. *United We Stand (The United Mine Workers of America 1890-1990)*. Washington: International Union, United Mine Workers of America, 1990.

Frank, David. Coal Masters and Coal Miners: Strikes and Roots of Class Conflict in the Cape Breton Coal Industry. MA thesis, Dalhousie University, 1971.

———. The Cape Breton Coal Industry and the Rise and Fall of the British Empire Steel Corporation. *Acadiensis* 7 (1977) (1): 3-34.

———. The Miner's Financier: Women in the Cape Breton Coal Towns, 1917. *Atlantis* 8 (1983) (2): 137-43.

———. Tradition and Culture in the Cape Breton Mining Community in the Early Twentieth Century. In *Cape Breton at 200: Historical Essays in Honour of the Island's Bicentennial, 1785-1985*, ed. Ken Donovan, 203-18. Sydney, NS: University College of Cape Breton Press, 1985.

———. The Industrial Folksong in Cape Breton. *Canadian Folklore Canadien* 8 (1986) (1-2): 21-42.

———. Working-Class Politics: The Election of J. B. McLachlan, 1916-1935. In *The Island: New Perspectives on Cape Breton History*, ed. Ken Donovan, 187-219. Fredericton, NB: Acadiensis Press, 1990.

———. The 1920s: Class and Region, Resistance and Accommodation. In *The Atlantic Provinces in Confederation*, ed. E. R. Forbes and D. A. Muise, 233-71. Toronto: University of Toronto Press, 1993.

———. *J. B. McLachlan: A Biography*. Toronto: James Lorimer Press, 1999.

Gray, FW. *Musings of a Maritime Miner*. Sydney: np, 1940.

Green, Archie. *Only a Miner*. Chicago: University of Illinois Press, 1972.

Handel, Johnny. *Johnny Handel Songbook*. Spin Publications, 1975.

Hornsby, Stephen. 1989. Staple Trades, Subsistence Agriculture, and Nineteenth-Century Cape Breton Island. *Annals of the Association of American Geographers* 79: 411-34.

———. *Nineteenth Century Cape Breton: A Historical Geography.* Montreal: McGill-Queen's University Press, 1992.

Korson, George. *Coal Dust on the Fiddle.* Hatboro: *Folklore Associates,* 1965.

———. *Minstrels of the Mine Patch.* Hatboro: Folklore Associates, 1964.

Lamey, Christina M. Davis Day through the Years: A Cape Breton Coalmining Tradition. *Nova Scotia Historical Review* 16 (1996): 23-33.

Lloyd, A L (*Ed*). *Coal dust Ballads.* London: Workers Music Association, 1951.

———. *Come All Ye Bold Miners.* London: Lawrence and Wishart, 1952.

———. *Singing Englishmen.* London: Workers Music Association, 1954.

MacDonald, Hugh R. *Trapper Boy.* Sydney: Cape Breton University Press, 2013.

MacEachern, Ron (ed). *Songs and Stories from Deep Cove, Cape Breton.* Sydney: College of Cape Breton Press, 1979.

MacGillivray, Allister. *Song for the Mira.* Sydney: New Dawn Enterprises, 1979.

———. *Diamonds in the Rough: Twenty-five Years with The Men of the Deeps.* Sydney: Men of the Deeps Music, 1991.

———. *The Men of the Deeps: The Continuing Saga*: Men of the Deeps Music, 2000.

MacGillivray, Allister and John C. O'Donnell. *The Cape Breton Song Collection.* Sydney: Sea-Cape Music, 1985.

———. *The Nova Scotia Song Collection.* Sydney: Sea-Cape Music, 1989.

MacGillivray, Donald. Cape Breton in the 1920s: A Community Besieged. In *Essays in Cape Breton History,* ed. Brian Tennyson, 49-67. Windsor, NS: Lancelot Press, 1973.

———. Military Aid to the Civil Power: The Cape Breton Experience in the 1920s. *Acadiensis* 3 (1974) (1): 45-64.

MacKenzie, Rennie. *BLAST! Cape Breton Mine Disasters.* Sydney: Breton Books, 2007.

———. 2008. http://www.seaside.ns.ca/~coalminer/index.html (accessed September 20, 2008).

MacKinnon, Richard. *Discovering Cape Breton Folklore.* Sydney: Cape Breton University Press, 2009.

———. A Typology of Cape Breton Island Company Housing. In *Company Houses, Company Towns: Heritage and Conservation,* 7-45. Ed. Andrew Molloy and Tom Urbaniak. Sydney, NS: CBU Press, 2016.

McCawley, Stuart. *Cape Breton Come-All-Ye.* Glace Bay: Brodie Press, 1929.

McKay, Ian. "By Wisdom, Wile or War": The Provincial Workmen's Association and the Struggle for Working-Class Independence in Nova Scotia, 1879-97. *Labour / Le Travail* 18 (1986): 12-62.

———. The Crisis of Dependent Development: Class Conflict in the Nova Scotia Coalfields, 1872-1876. *The Canadian Journal of Sociology / Cahiers canadiens de sociologie* 13 (1988): 9-48.

Mellor, John. *The Company Store.* Toronto: Doubleday Canada, 1983.

Millward, Hugh. Mine Locations and the Sequence of Coal Exploitation on the Sydney Coalfield, 1720-1980. In *Cape Breton at 200: Historical Essays in Honour of the Island's Bicentennial, 1785-1985,* ed. Ken Donovan, 183-202. Sydney, NS: University College of Cape Breton Press, 1985.

Muise, Del. The Making of an Industrial Community: Cape Breton Coal Towns, 1867-1900. In *Cape Breton Historical Essays,* ed. Don MacGillivray and Brian Tennyson, 76-94. Sydney, NS: College of Cape Breton Press, 1980.

News of the Universe: Poems of Twofold Consciousness. San Francisco.

Newton, David. *Where Coal Is King. The Story of the Cape Breton Miners' Museum.* Glace Bay: Cape Breton Miners' Foundation, Quarry Point. 1992.

O'Donnell, John C. *The Men of the Deeps Songbook.* Waterloo, Ontario: Waterloo Music Company, 1975.

———. *And Now the Fields are Green. A Collection of Coal Mining Songs in Canada.* Sydney: University College of Cape Breton Press, 1992.

———. *The Music of The Men of the Deeps.* Antigonish: Amberglade Music, 2009.

———. "Blackleg Miners in Cape Breton," *Canadian Folk Music Bulletin,* 18 (3) 1984.

———. "Towards a Collection of Coal Mining Songs in Canada," *Canadian Folk Music Journal,* 1984.

———. "Industrial songs as part of a culture," *International Journal of Music Education,* 6, 1985.

———. "Labour's cultural impact on the community," *Canadian Folk Music Journal,* 14. 1986.

———. "The contribution of American folklorists to research in music of Canadian coal mining communities," in Dorothy Moore and James Morrison (eds), *Work, Ethnicity, and Oral History.* Halifax: Saint Mary's University International Education Centre, Issues in Ethnicity and Multiculturalism series, 1988.

———. "Join the Union or You'll Die." *Canadian Folklore Canadien,* 14 (2) 1993.

_____ "Music as an Expression of Culture in the Mining Communities of Cape Breton Island," *Canadian Issues*, Aug/Sept 2001, 29.

Petrie, Daniel, dir. *The Bay Boy*, film. Daniel Petrie, prod., 1986.

Petrie, Harry. Tab for the Dominion Coal Company Limited's Store No. 14, 20 July 1918 to 22 July 1918. New Waterford Historical Society Archives, New Waterford, Nova Scotia.

Seeger, Peggy. "And Now The Fields are Green." *English Folk Music Journal*, 6 (5) 1994.

Thomas, Philip. *Songs of the Pacific Northwest*. Saanichton: Hancock House Publications. 1979.

UNESCO *International Convention for the Safeguarding of the Intangible Cultural Heritage*, 17 October 2003.

Vincent, Pierre. *Real V. Benoit, Le Seoul chanter underground Canadian*: Le Compositeur Canadien, no 76, January 1973.

Walsh, Lillian Crewe. *Calling Cape Breton*. np, nd.

Williston, Floyd. *Johnny Miles: Nova Scotia's Marathon King*. Halifax: Nimbus, 1990.

Zodrow, Erwin L., Christopher J. Cleal and Barry A. Thomas. *An Amateur's Guide to Coal-Plant Fossils on Cape Breton Island, Nova Scotia, Canada*. Cape Breton University Press, 2001.

About the Author

John C. O'Donnell is Professor Emeritus and former Chair of the Department of Music at St. Francis Xavier University in Antigonish, Nova Scotia, having retired from active teaching in September 2000. Professor O'Donnell holds degrees in music from Gonzaga University in Spokane, Washington, and the University of London (England) Kings College.

For most of the past fifty years Jack O'Donnell has also served as conductor and musical director of Cape Breton's coal miners choir, The Men of the Deeps, a position which required him to travel almost weekly from Antigonish to Glace Bay in order to coach and rehearse the singing miners. Under his leadership the choir has performed throughout most of Canada and the United States, and in 1976 The Men of the Deeps became the first Canadian performing group to tour the People's Republic of China following the restoration of diplomatic relations between the two nations.

In 1983 Professor O'Donnell's efforts were honoured by the government of Canada when he was awarded the Order of Canada, this nation's highest civilian award. And in 1993 his efforts were recognized by Cape Breton University with the degree Doctor of Letters, *honoris causa* – an honour that was bestowed upon the entire membership of The Men of the Deeps in the year 2000. Jack's long association with Cape Breton's coal miners choir was again recognized in 2013 when, in conjunction with the 300 year anniversary celebrations of Fortress Louisbourg, Cape Breton University's Beaton Institute presented him with the inaugural Katharine McLennan Award honouring his contributions to the heritage of Cape Breton's coal mining communities.

In 2015 he received special recognition from his peers when the East Coast Music Association presented him with the Helen Creighton Lifetime Achievement Award at it annual awards ceremony in Sydney.

Professor O'Donnell has published widely on the subject of coal mining songs in Canada, contributing regularly to several national and international journals. He has also published two books documenting the songs of The Men of the Deeps and has collaborated with singer/songwriter Allister MacGillivray on two of MacGillivray's major collections: *The Cape Breton Song Collection* and *The Nova Scotia Song Collection* (Sydney, Sea Cape Music Limited, 1985 and 1989). In 1992 he completed a major anthology of songs related to the coal mining industry, *And Now the Fields are Green: A Collection of Coal Mining Songs in Canada* (Sydney, NS, University College of Cape Breton Press).

www.ingramcontent.com/pod-product-compliance
Lightning Source LLC
Chambersburg PA
CBHW080509110426
42742CB00017B/3049